FRIENDS OF ALICE PUBLISHING

A WOMAN ALONE

ISABEL DEL RIO is a British-Spanish writer and linguist. Born in Madrid, she has lived in London most of her life. She has published fiction and poetry in both English and Spanish. Her books include *La duda*, shortlisted for two literary awards in Spain, and the bilingual *Zero Negative–Cero negativo*. Her latest collections of short stories are *Paradise & Hell* and *Una muerte incidental;* her recent novels are *El tiempo que falta* and *Dissent*; and her latest poetry collection is *Dolorem Ipsum*.

A Woman Alone is Isabel's very personal memoir.

A Woman Alone

Copyright © 2021 Isabel del Rio. All Rights Reserved.

Cover design: Isabel del Rio
Photography: Isabel del Rio
Publishing rights:
FRIENDS OF ALICE PUBLISHING
London W5 5BX, United Kingdom
www.friendsofalice.com

Any unauthorised copying or reproduction of content or text without the written permission from the author or the publisher is strictly prohibited.

All rights reserved

FRIENDS OF ALICE
- PUBLISHING -

ISBN - 978-1-9160306-8-8

ISABEL DEL RIO

A WOMAN ALONE

FRAGMENTS OF A MEMOIR

London, 2021

FRIENDS OF ALICE PUBLISHING

To Sussie and Julia: they already knew *when* and *where*, but they have now asked *why* and *how*

"Autobiography is much too grand a word. It suggests a purposeful study of one's whole life. It implies names, times, places in tidy chronological order. What I want is to plunge my hand into a lucky dip and come up with a handful of assorted memories... And though I do not expect to be able to keep up with chronological continuity, I can at least try to begin at the beginning."
Agatha Christie, 'An Autobiography' (1977)

"Hasta la adolescencia, la memoria tiene más interés en el futuro que en el pasado, así que mis recuerdos del pueblo no estaban todavía idealizados por la nostalgia."
Gabriel García Márquez, 'Vivir para contarla' (2003)

Notes

This memoir was written in English, except for quotes and excerpts in Spanish (in *italics*).

The initials of all those mentioned here have been changed.

A few sections in this memoir are taken (not necessarily verbatim) from the more autobiographical elements in my books 'Zero Negative', 'Ataraxy', 'Madrid, Madrid, Madrid', 'El tiempo que falta', 'Punto de fuga' and 'Dolorem Ipsum'.

Here are then the fragments of a life; as in a shipwreck, I salvaged what I could.

In the beginning was a whole sentence. And the sentence was: "And now we'll try for a boy!" Yes, that is what they said when I was born: *"¡Y ahora iremos a por el niño!"* Luckily for them, a boy followed eighteen months later.

I started my life as a typical product of a particularly difficult period in history, and I suppose many can lay claim to similar beginnings. In my case, I was born in a country besieged by the social and political struggles that followed one of the bloodiest civil wars in the last century, the Spanish Civil War. If wars usually end with a peace agreement, however one-sided, civil wars –sister against sister, brother against brother– never seem to reach a clear-cut conclusion. In this case, the war was followed by decades of trauma and suffering and, with the winning side determined to obliterate the losing side and all it symbolised, reconciliation and forgiveness would be difficult to attain.

But let me tell you all this before I forget.

From the start, my motto must have been *"¡Cuanto antes, mejor!"* No wonder I was a premature baby. As I saw it, there was never enough time, and I would always be in a frantic hurry. Well before the agreed hour, I arrived in whatever places I needed to be. I would get to airports at dawn to catch a midday plane. I would deride those who were late or who squandered time in needless activities, such as games or pastimes. I could be seen running to get from one place to the next when there was no need, climbing stairs at speed, circling around the house as fast as I could when doing chores and tidying up. Time opposed everything I stood for, putting an end to things far too early and, worst of all, cutting short the lives of those I loved. It was clearly my enemy, Time was, and I steered well clear of it by being faster than it could ever be.

I tried to keep all these recollections alive by reliving them in my mind time and time again, always afraid to let go in case I would forget them. It appears, though, that when you try to remember events, you do not recall the original happening but the successive memories of it. It could then be claimed that, over time, I accrued several life stories, depending on when I retold a memory, how and to whom; a little like recounting the lives of several people who would probably not recognise each other were they to cross paths. My hope was that piecing together a narrative from such diverse material might provide a sense of wholeness. And yet, a composite picture of who you are, superimposing all those versions of yourself, might shock you into the realisation that you have been living with a total stranger all along.

Mírame. ¿Es que soy transparente, es que no existo, es que no me quieres?

Now that I have become so inquisitive about my beginnings, there is no one around to ask about my early years, no hospital records, no living doctors or midwives or nurses to check with, certainly no relatives from the previous generation. But I was told that as a premature baby I looked weak, small, scrawny. I was not placed in an incubator as I should have been; incubators were available at the time but probably not yet in use in the Madrid hospital where I was born. For a new-born that had still not reached full-term, I was ill-equipped to face the world, yet was expected to either get on with it or perish. But what contributed even more to such a precipitous entry into this world was that my birth turned out to be traumatic: it was a breech birth. Nowadays a Caesarean delivery is performed in most breech presentations. But back then, with no ultrasound and no developments like, say, the Webster technique, moxibustion or ECVs, you were expected to survive on your own without any outside help. In my case, the first thing to put an appearance was not the head, with the mat of blonde hair that I had then, and not the face, with its crumpled expression of incredulity after having been violently pushed out into the world, but a little toe setting out on the long path that awaited me.

... a lo largo de una noche inconsolable las reflexiones se suceden sin orden aparente y sin que sirvan para aclarar nada, y las observo con atención como si fueran el producto de otros sin atreverme a declararme su dueña y señora, y de a poco van saliéndome de la boca las palabras que corresponden a cada una de ellas en sucesión y sin hacer apenas ruido, para decir justamente lo que jamás imaginé que sabía...

Grandfather concocted a unique name for me from my three official names, and that is how I was known by the family, and still am. *Ma* from María, *be* from Isabel, *lia* from Julia. As a youngster, I always felt that I was two girls: one, the girl with the official name; and the other, the real girl with a very different name. I was so embarrassed when friends or teachers found out that my family had a special name for me, and this was always a source of great anxiety. It became a secret that I did not want divulged, a revelation about my real identity that was not to be shared with anyone outside my closest circle. To this day, I still experience an inexplicable embarrassment about my real name, the real me.

A flor de piel: there is no particular reason why I am including this expression here; it is just that I very much like how it looks on paper and how it sounds, and I will use any occasion to say it.

I was never fully of where I should be, for I thought I was living a parallel imaginary life instead of my real life; this is now called lack of awareness, of presence, of mindfulness. Plus, I would constantly think that I should have been someone else instead of who I was: different, better, more interesting; this is now called lack of self-esteem, self-confidence, self-respect.

Mother and I were both first at something: she, a first-timer; and me, a first-born. I seem to have thrived despite that challenging beginning, born both premature and breech, and I remember someone telling me that I sucked milk at such an extraordinary rate that within a little over a month I was larger than I would have otherwise been, had I remained *in utero* as was my right.

"La vida da muchas vueltas" Mother used to claim when talking about life's twists and turns. She repeated this saying on a regular basis, as if walking in circles herself.

Throughout this memoir I talk about the impact that the Spanish Civil War had on members of my family. May the first mention here be the last declaration of the war, produced by the insurgents upon the ending of hostilities. Dated 1st of April 1939, and called *último parte*, the declaration included a minimum number of words for maximum effect, beginning with a simple enough statement: *En el día de hoy*. Then, under the guise of language imbued with rogue literary aspirations, an ablative absolute was used to give the sentence some gravity in the style of ancient rhymes, with the opposing and legitimate army described by using the term 'red' as per the terminology in use by the winning and illegitimate side: *cautivo y desarmado el ejército rojo*. The declaration goes on to announce the military success by the victors: *han alcanzado las tropas nacionales sus últimos objetivos militares*, a sentence with the noun placed after the verb for effect, stylistically almost apologetic of the noun, as if shielding it from accusations of wrongdoing. *La guerra ha terminado*: this is the final affirmation, without specifying for whom it has ended, nor what has started in its place; in any case, the atrocities, terror and senselessness would continue for decades. And to close, the garish signature: *El Generalísimo*, the dictator-to-be signing his name with a totalitarian superlative.

Es indiscutible que todo se reduce a un juego, aunque también sabemos lo necesario que es jugar...

My breech birth was always remembered by family members as a feat –whether my mother's feat or mine they never specified. They would also recall how my mother had suffered horribly because of the experience, and how it left her with no desire whatsoever for any further progeny, promising to never have another child. Such a promise would not be kept for long, and some months later Mother became pregnant again. In evolutionary terms, if women remembered the pain they felt during childbirth, we would reproduce once and only once. Mother never once talked to me about my delivery, and I always felt that she held something against me. It was probably the unbearable pain of my breech birth.

It turned out that I was the child of parents who were on opposing sides during the war: Father in *Castilla la Vieja*, the fascist stronghold; and Mother in *Catalunya*, to where her family had migrated, and which defended the Republic to the very end. The course of both their lives changed with time, sometimes beyond recognition. To save what she called her soul, Mother eventually turned to religion; on his part, Father soon fathomed that military force was not the route to what he would call the salvation of the soul. Whatever the soul was, it became the guiding light in their life stories.

For someone who believes in the power of make-believe, it was only right that I should fall in love with those who resembled heroes, and I never saw such look-alikes for what they were but only as the available version of a dream.

In those days there was low survival expectancy. Most breech babies died at birth, with their neck snapping when they were pushed out into the world. They used to say that you are as lucky as someone born breech: *"Tienes más suerte que si hubieras nacido de pie."* Yes, I was fortunate to be alive; despite all, I made it. Yes, I somehow made it. This was to be the rule throughout: I somehow made it; and somehow, I will make it. Always by a whisker and by a second, I badly needed to hit the ground running, and how I used to run throughout my life. And then one recent summer's day, I was forced to stop in my tracks and had to learn to do things unhurriedly and deliberately, with full awareness and presence. This is how it happened: there seemed to be no other way of preventing me from speeding so much in every direction, so my physical body first demanded and then, as I took no measures to slow down, dramatically imposed a standstill. But more of that later.

Catastrophism: until I knew that word, I could not understand what the problem was.

Dressed like a bride at age eight, I closed my eyes and opened my mouth. I felt the round white sliver of unleavened bread placed on my tongue. That holiest of communions turned out to be a highly ornate story, not unlike the fairy stories that I would read at night. You had to suspend your disbelief (and trust instead in the invisible and the inaudible); the setting was epic (the magnificent school chapel in my London prep school); the characters, dramatic (the robes of the priest worthy of the most theatrical enterprise); the language, lyrical (from a book written so long ago that it had gone through the gentle and wise hands of endless translators, elders and propagandists, all of whom embellished it time and time again, with the purpose of persuading readers to believe in a mind-blowing kingdom in the skies). I suppose that, in those days, I believed everything I was told without raising a single doubt. And yet on the day of the Holy Communion I could not understand, for no one had explained it to me convincingly enough, why I was swallowing a small piece of unleavened bread on its own when that mid-morning I was feeling so very hungry; or worse still, why I was dressed as a bride if there was no bridegroom around.

Monsieur Lefort travelled on business from Paris to Valladolid and fell in love with my great-great-grandmother. He never returned to his country, for his new wife did not wish to leave her hometown; and he certainly did not want to be parted from her, not even for a few days. He became thus a Frenchman without a nation for he never identified with his country of adoption, nor learnt Spanish suitably, making endless grammatical mistakes and speaking with a very heavy French accent until the day he died. His love for his Spanish wife was so much more significant than any notions he would have had of country, language, culture, history and nationality.

Such are the words by Cervantes that keep me going: *"Todas estas borrascas que nos suceden son señales de que presto ha de serenar el tiempo y han de sucedernos bien las cosas, porque no es posible que el mal ni el bien sean durables, y de aquí se sigue que, habiendo durado mucho el mal, el bien está ya cerca."*

Mother did not attend prenatal classes, had no check-ups, and never knew that the baby inside her was growing the wrong way round. When she was taken to hospital, the surgeon said to Father: *"No me responsabilizo ni de la madre ni de la criatura."* Father shook his head to avoid a heated reaction, his dream of a wife and a child fading before his eyes, just like all his other dreams. Putting on the thick rubber gloves used at the time (and which would nowadays only be used for washing-up), the surgeon scolded Father severely and asked why they had not come to see him earlier, for he could have examined Mother and prevented a disaster. And when Father was about to justify his lack of action and, more importantly, his lack of knowledge about bearing and rearing children, the surgeon went into the operating theatre with a heavily pregnant Mother to determine whether one man's dream was worth saving.

My public admission: I can be vain, shallow, temperamental, conceited, naive.

One of my earliest recollections: I was certain that if you imagined the worst, it would not happen, for the simple reason that only the unexpected occurred. When I became older and recognised the fallacy, I proved time and time again that things did not work like that in the real world. And yet, despite the overwhelming evidence, today I still imagine the worst before any event.

I was born in a hospital in Carabanchel, the working-class district where the battle for Madrid was fought.

Built by political prisoners, not so much imprisoned as enslaved, the megalomaniac *Valle de los Caídos* erected in the outskirts of Madrid shakes your entrails when you see it appear in the middle of the spectacular *Sierra de Guadarrama*. From the gargantuan cross to the enormous hands of the four Gospel writers, this monument to the fallen was built after the end of the civil war under exceptionally harsh conditions. Prisoners were promised shorter sentences in exchange for the building of this monstrosity, and over the 18 years it took to build it almost 27,000 died in the process. Antonio Machado had anticipated the catastrophic results of the war when he wrote: *"Una de las dos Españas ha de helarte el corazón."* Those were the verses I remembered when once –and only once– I visited the place.

It is just that some stories do not have a beginning, an end and a middle.

And the surgeon, briefly coming out of the operating theatre after having examined Mother, again confirmed that the situation was dire: *"No puedo prometer que la criatura o la madre saldrán con vida de ésta."* And Father once more held his temper and thought about the various possibilities: both his wife and his child would die, or only his wife, or perhaps only his child. The choice between the two of us, mother and baby, would have been me, since the Catholic Church dictated that in such life-or-death cases the child had to be saved at any cost because, otherwise, you could be depriving the Church of a saint. By that same token, you might be saving society from a mass murderer –that is what I would think as a young girl when learning the dogmas, but this particular idea I never voiced in public at the time.

On a day like today I am mostly writing in survival mode.

Since lockdown, days appear to be so much alike. Soon we will have to call *today*, *yesterday* and *tomorrow* by a common name, for we can hardly distinguish between them anymore. Each day starts and ends on a very similar note: at home, with the same person or persons, repeating the same series of actions, engaging with outsiders solely on a computer screen or from afar. Even what is squeezed between morning and night diverges little from one day to the next. Things are seen in a similarly dull light and our mood is, if anything, even more despondent from week to week, with little hope of betterment. But whether this state of affairs goes on for longer or it soon comes to an end, we will have the same two options that we have always had when facing a new day: to stay put or to graciously disappear.

... lo que no vi porque estaba mirando hacia otro lado, lo que no viví, lo que pude haber pedido y no pedí, lo que pude haber sido y jamás fui, lo que no supe, lo que me perdí...

When it came to things that she felt very close to, or even things that she was reluctant to acknowledge, she always addressed herself as *she* and not as *I*.

The beginning of a teenager's war diary, as written by Mother:
19 de julio de 1936*: Hoy ha estallado la Revolución en España. Es una lucha entre ricos y pobres, obreros y propietarios. De aquí de Barcelona, pronto hemos ahuyentado a los fascistas, y los pocos generales que se han hecho fuertes en los cuarteles han sido abandonados por sus soldados. En la toma del cuartel de Atarazanas, ha muerto un gran pensador anarquista, Francisco Ascaso. El pueblo sediento de venganza contra el yugo y la tiranía de los que hasta hoy les tenían esclavizados se ha lanzado a la calle y, cual un huracán desencadenado, han matado a todo el que se oponía a su libertad.*
Día 20*: Desde todas las iglesias y centros catequísticos, los soldados han pretendido hacerse fuertes inútilmente. Las iglesias han sido quemadas sin quedar de ellas nada que recuerde el pasado.*
Día 21*: El castillo de Montjuïc ha sido tomado por los leales, y sus cañones han ayudado eficazmente a lograr la victoria.*
Día 25*: Catalunya es nuestra. De aquí se dirigen al frente de Zaragoza muchos hombres.*
Día 27*: No nos falta nada de comestibles. De todas formas, hay cola para comprar pan. Yo bajo a ella, y de repente desde una terraza nos empiezan a disparar. Afortunadamente no dan en el blanco, pero nos refugiamos*

en el horno, y ya desde allí oímos un tiroteo endiablado entre algún fascista que está escondido y nuestros milicianos.
Día 30: *Los milicianos son un ejército formado por el pueblo.*
Día 02: *Todo ha acabado. Y no se oye ni el más pequeño signo que delate que estamos en estado de guerra...*

Aged six, I penned little stories and illustrated them. Father would boast about my childish productions and show them to his friends and colleagues. When I was older, he would use my name for the stories he sent to various literary competitions and publishers. The reason was that, as an officer, he was not allowed to do anything other than his job. I once asked him: what would happen if your stories were ever to be selected in one of those competitions and the judges found out that the author was me, a mere fourteen-year-old? Father said that he would deal with that sort of thing when the time came. But the time never came, unhappily. And now I am thinking of doing something similar with my own children, given my age and, mostly, my anguish.

In my twenties, I married in a cream-coloured bridal gown. When I married again, decades later, I was dressed in silver. It was like going through the stages of life, from youthful brilliant off-white tones, almost not there, to mature silvery hues, all finished and done. In between there have been various associations, we could call them, but none important enough to mention, certainly no significant others. Oh, I lie: one taught me about Art, as he aspired to be an artist at my expense; another taught me about the human psyche, attempting to psychoanalyse me as a fascinating case for his files as opposed to being merely captivated by me; another confirmed that he was not interested in the whole woman because what he wanted was, and I quote, to cut me in pieces; and another finally admitted that his regular amorous declarations ("you and me against the world" and that sort of thing) were really meant to alienate me completely from my loved ones. As I said earlier, nothing too important to mention.

Enlightened verses by Sor Juana Inés de la Cruz: "*En perseguirme, Mundo, ¿qué interesas? / ¿En qué te ofendo, cuando sólo intento / poner bellezas en mi entendimiento / y no mi entendimiento en las bellezas?*"

At the beginning of the pandemic, I overstocked with everything imaginable. I even fashioned a kind of field hospital at the top floor of the house in case one of us got sick and needed to isolate. It had all kinds of medical supplies and health products, from a variety of over-the-counter medications to bandages, from a good supply of toothpaste to an even better supply of talcum-powder. I truly thought that the pandemic would be the beginning of the end and, worse, that we would never go back to our regular and mostly predictable life. As of today, I still think along those lines, and this is why I have not yet dismantled my field hospital.

Grandmother taught me how to use four-letter words without causing too much offence, and she would say *concho* instead of *coño*. Grandfather used to repeat *me cago en diez* at the drop of a hat, satisfied that it was a more polite version than the original; he was, of course, being respectful in that he did not take the name of God in vain, even though he did not believe a word about heavenly creatures. In fact, whenever Grandfather came across one of his enemies in the street (of which he had many in the world of business in his day), he would exclaim: *"¡Es uno de los diez!"*

After years of having avoided the temptation of reviewing her life simply because she suspected that any such review would not be as pleasurable as most temptations are, it is now time to confront and reflect and conclude, and finally put her house in order.

Más resultó en menos, mucho se convirtió en poco, crecer fue perecer, tanto se quedó en nada...

In my third decade, I produced a child with golden hair, and in my fourth decade, I produced a child with raven hair.

With my hand on my heart, I can honestly say that I had a more or less happy childhood. This does not mean that I was well prepared for the dramas that were to unravel later on, as we shall see.

And so, she cannot look at sweet things any more without thinking that they will turn sour one day.

After giving birth to me, Mother developed hyperthyroidism, probably because of a serious lack of iodine. It was, after all, the aftermath of the war, with its abysmal hunger and its desperate shortages of everything from food to justice. She eventually had a goitre operation and after that she always wore a necklace to conceal her scar, even during the hottest summer days. Her favourite necklace was made of red coral, each fine coral tooth conveniently masking the vestiges of the many long stiches that encircled her neck. Yes, she always tried desperately to conceal everything that was going on in her life, from scars to sadness.

In those days, things were done to either please or appease others, and the question Mother asked before doing anything was: "What will people think?"

My story is told as remembered; at this age, though, the train of thought appears to derail sporadically.

My standards were exacting, flawless. You just have to look at those old photographs or short films of me. I was the illusion of a child, hardly flesh and blood; in fact, more a pretty china doll or a faultless and sweet automaton. And such were the beliefs imposed on the child that I was then: if you got too close, the ground would make you filthy; at any time, you could fall and hurt yourself beyond repair; dust might be jam-packed with microbes. All this instilled in me a fear of dirt and grime and, worst of all, an abhorrence of imperfection. Here is the result for you to see.

I hold all these memories to be nothing but true and real, but then I cannot seek conclusive confirmation of what happened, for there are no survivors from most of the episodes told, places have disappeared, ideas have been superseded.

Recently there was an unforeseen episode that critically shook me in my entrails, forcing me to both review and renew: I suffered a series of blows to the system, doctors call them cerebrovascular accidents. Like all unexpected events, it was an experience that would radically change me; in fact, once the ischaemic episodes began to subside, I felt that I had become a different woman. I would not go as far as talking pupas and butterflies, of course, that would be presumptuous. But I am referring to a juncture in evolutionary terms: not a sudden mutation but a necessary makeover when survival demands a major change in a human's life. It took me time to recover, not that you ever recover completely from certain experiences, mostly in your mind. But in its own strange way, this medical episode forced me to re-evaluate in depth who I was and, particularly, to reassess how I had lived out my life until then. All of which meant that I finally started to write my story in my very own words.

I was born with what looked deliciously like a strawberry on my head, though not the kind you eat with cream. The strawberry was most probably a dermoid cyst, with no one saying anything of the sort at the time. In those old days the truth was deliberately withheld, especially in the case of a new-born baby girl, which was not the gender expected or desired for a first-born. And then, ever so delicately so as not to trouble the parents of that uninvited female creature, doctors did not call the growth a cyst but, yes, a strawberry. All parties naturally knew the truth about the cyst but decided instead to keep to that facile fairy-tale narrative, as if life might be made more agreeable with a touch of fantasy than with outright facts. In photographs, you can see that for a whole year I lived with that strawberry –such a kind euphemism for a pink cyst– on my head. From the stories reported to me, the strawberry was removed when I started to walk, aged one. Whether the removal of my strawberry was linked to the relevant psychomotor development, I will never know. But I have generally had good coordination, if little interest in sports and activities that require huge physical exertion. In the course of the operation to remove the cyst, not only did the make-believe strawberry disappear, but also a small piece of my skull, luckily behind the hairline. I suppose the surgeons dug well into the brain in case the whole thing was malignant. So yes, I have a small dip in my head, not visible to the naked eye, but very much there if you happen to run your finger along the left side of my scalp. Does that mean that a section of my brain did not develop fully or become less furrowed than it ought to be? My constant dissatisfaction, my urge for wandering, my expectation for things that are not to be found readily anywhere, all this could perhaps be attributed to the fact that my brain was interfered with at a young age, medically speaking. But it could also be that, somehow and in a much more down-to-earth way, I have always been, you could say, pining for my long-lost strawberry. To this day, I still talk about my strawberry *("¡Mi fresa!")* and not about the cyst on my head. Obviously, misnaming something is not as bad as misdiagnosing. The misdiagnoses came later, just wait.

She tried to fill the emotional void by being so very over-attached to inanimate objects, mostly family mementoes. Eventually she tweaked that people cannot be replaced with things, but then neither can things be replaced with people.

A boy did follow me to this Earth. Father and Mother tried very hard to get pregnant again when I was still a-suckling, and they got their boy. The loveliest, kindest, funniest boy. My companion-in-arms, my dear Brother.

On his last day before leaving London and returning to Greece, L invited me to his apartment for a farewell meeting. He also invited the woman with whom he had been having a separate affair, without her or me knowing about the other. Me, the younger but darker woman; and she, the older but blonde lover. The two of us had been invited at the same time; it was all terribly civilised. L had been cheating on both of us, yet there we all were on the last day of his stay in the city and the country, behaving impeccably and having tea and scones. If I had slept with him, it was because he was a Nureyev lookalike and not because of his lacklustre lovemaking. I wonder if I also reminded him of anyone, possibly Irene Papas. Ah, if only.

Among all the many objects that I lost along the way, I most miss an early edition of 'Pinocchio' by Carlo Collodi, in the original version. The book was published in 1892 after Collodi died (the author would never know how successful his work became). It had been promised to me by Grandfather, and I would read it whenever I went to visit him at his house. Whoever has the book now, can you please, please, please return it.

In case you are wondering, I have lived almost three quarters of my life in the UK, and only one quarter in Spain: the first seven years in Madrid – then I lived in London until I was a teenager – and then I lived in Madrid once again: ten years there, dreaming almost every night that I would return to London, until eventually I did. Call it a dream come true, if you like, but it would be more accurate to say that it was one long-drawn-out announcement of what would inevitably happen one day.

With a sense of loss and on the edge of defeat, still she goes on.

During the war, a grenade exploded on his back and horribly injured his right arm. Whilst recovering, Father had to resort to using his left arm, something he was not entirely unfamiliar with. You see, he had been left-handed as a child, but at school he was forced to use his right hand, with his left hand tied behind his back. *"¡Así se escribe con propiedad!"* the teacher would say every morning when tying Father's hand. And if he complained, he would be hit with a thick wooden ruler, following the intonation of: *"¡La letra con sangre entra!"*

What have I been up to during the pandemic? Me? So many activities: doing arm and shoulder exercises as well as leg and foot exercises to help me recover; trying to get my speech back in working order; practising daily meditation to avoid the worry of further ischaemic episodes; going for walks, at first a little awkwardly but later on at speed; trying to remember to take my medication on time; reading unendingly; playing castanets and wind drum; juggling soft balls; watercolour-painting; tapestry-making; pencil-sketching; photographing almost everything around me on my iPhone; wondering about the options I have left in my life, if any. Ah, I forget the most important thing of all: writing in earnest.

First inklings of death happened early. My parents took me to visit a young second cousin, ill with polio. She was called Luz, like her mother and her grandmother. It was probably assumed that by then the child was not infectious because it was very sadly the end of the road for her; in hindsight, visiting contagious patients was an extremely dangerous thing to do, especially when it involved young children as visitors. A year older than me, my cousin's waxen face had a rigid but tender smile. In that large and mostly bare hospital room, the little girl was lying in her bed, unable to move and tightly wrapped in what already looked like a shroud. There seemed to be an iridescent light shining on her face as if in a Christmas play. I was sure that at any moment she would remove the covers and jump up and start playing with me. Or better still: flap her wings, because she looked like the image I had of angels in my tiny guiltless mind, and thus she has remained all these years. But it was not a happy ending: the following week I was told that she had died. Died? At that age I did not know what death was or that it even existed, and yet it was thrown at me like a pile of mud. No one had ever explained a thing about death, for life was supposed to last forever, everything was. Worst of all was that I had to confront a new idea which shook me to the core: death could happen to anyone at any given time, whatever your age, dreams, or hopes.

I placed a bell on the floor beside my bed so that if I suffered another stroke, this time in the middle of the night, I would ring the bell and alert everyone in the house. Is there also, I wonder, a bell for fear, for disquiet, for agitation?

Mother's favourite game? The *what-ifs*. Am I playing this game as well, resorting to conjecture to make up for the discontent in one's present life? This *what-if* is a useful expression to invent improbable stories, like what if I developed wings, what if language was one day considered superfluous, what if our planet stopped rotating. What if I had married my first love instead of marrying your Father, Mother would repeat. *"Ay, si me hubiera casado con él y no con tu padre..."*

Spanish by birth and British by upbringing, with some French blood thrown in for effect. But to be more precise, you could also describe her as a perpetual outsider.

Desde mis días de estudiante siempre he pensado que morir era una asignatura pendiente...

When he was young, Father believed that women were not creatures of this world, but angel-like and perfect, incapable of producing anything ugly like secretions or, God forbid, excretions. One day Father noticed a dark hair growing on a woman's leg, and that made him rethink the delusion he had been brought up to believe; but only for a while because, after falling desperately in love with Mother and not being able to have sex with her for several years of engagement until they married, he soon went back to seeing women as belonging to a world that had little to do with this one. I think that he never completely gave up those outlandish ideas. Thus, such expectations placed on me would always be completely beyond my reach.

Grieving was done as follows: the first year, you were supposed to dress totally in black, *luto riguroso*; the second year, you wore dark colours, *alivio de luto*; the third year, you wore clothes that were discreet and modest. And on the fourth year, you could go back to wearing your usual clothes but nothing that would attract too much attention. Of course, there was inner grieving, which in my case was of the darkest ever hue.

As mentioned, at age five I learnt of the death of my very young cousin Luz from polio. Aged eight, a very mischievous little boy called Arturito, who was from my group of young friends in Madrid; he loved climbing lampposts and was electrocuted in one of his climbs. Aged ten I was told about the death of my young uncle Manuel, who saved a boy from being suffocated in a grain silo and died heroically. My beloved Grandfather sadly died when I was thirteen, but it was somehow expected because of his age and illness. Aged fourteen, three school friends and three nuns from school died when the coach in which they were travelling fell down a precipice in Puerto de Pajares; I was supposed to go on that trip, but days before the departure my parents decided against it. And then aged sixteen, the unforeseen happened: I experienced true, definitive, unshakeable, unspeakable, cruel death for the first time; my most powerful memory from that episode was seeing Mother's shut eyes inside the casket.

Virginity I lost at twenty, so much later than anyone here. I do not believe it to be as valuable as some people like to think it is, but plainly an inconvenience. How things have changed: nowadays, virginity is what gives someone a bad name.

My first word, when I was nine months old, was the English word *girl*, even though in those days I was solely immersed in Spanish. It appears that I started at a young age to uphold who I was, although at times I totally failed as we shall see.

I did a bit of drama in my time: Lorca, Artaud, Weiss, Jarry. But regarding the dramas I had to live through, I shall give no names but only initials.

What happens is that I go out with a boy to our local park. The boy will become a famous poet in due course, but for now he is just a young lad. He seems clever and knowledgeable but is not at all good-looking. The main thing is that I like his company and he seems to like mine. We have fun in the park, walking and discussing school and books. And then he accompanies me home. We chat at the marbled entrance hall of the large block of flats in Madrid where I live. Just chatting, of course, I am fifteen at the time; you are not supposed to do more than that, no kissing or touching or suggesting anything that would be considered inappropriate back then. And suddenly, like a thunderbolt, Mother appears in the hall of the entrance to the house; from the balcony, she had seen us arriving and had rushed downstairs. She looks extremely alarmed and tells me in no uncertain terms to go upstairs, without so much as a 'Hello' or 'Good Evening' to the boy. I obey immediately, without saying goodbye to him. I have been totally humiliated, but so has the boy; as expected, he will never ask me out again, nor even say hello if we meet in the street. And when back at home, Mother angrily tells me off. She talks endlessly about how I should behave as a proper young girl and says: *"¿Qué van a pensar los vecinos?"* And I ask about what. And she replies that I was talking to a boy at the entrance of the house when I was not even engaged to him. *"¿Qué va a pensar la gente?"* she repeats, voicing centuries-old prejudices.

I was born with one mother tongue. But aged seven, I acquired a second one just like that. Each mother tongue arrives with a fresh set of thoughts and desires and beliefs, requiring me to be a different person when speaking one or the other. Both languages fight furiously within me to control the situation and establish the rules. Who am I, I would ask, this one or that one? *¿Ésta o ésa?*

Even when humbly collecting the grapes that had fallen on the ground from the vine in our garden, I would be an exquisitely dressed little girl with a red cape to match my shoes and protect me from all evils that happened to exist in our patch of greenery.

When I was growing up, people freely gave me their idea of what life was: *La vida es una lucha, un tango, una locura, un misterio, una absurdez, un carnaval, una injusticia, un sueño, una condena, un atropello, una quimera, un cuento, una canción, un milagro, una sorpresa, una mierda, una aventura, un experimento, una alegría, una maldición, un camino, un disparate, un prodigio, una verbena, un don, una tómbola, un hastío, una jodienda, un infierno, una canción, una arbitrariedad, un instante, una fiesta, una joya, una partida de ajedrez, un aburrimiento, una aventura, un drama, una maravilla, una engañifa, una cabronada, un juego, un minuto, un viaje, una tómbola, un castigo, una novela, una suerte, un acertijo, una puta, un golpe bajo, una injusticia, una carrera de obstáculos, un regalo, una bendición, un encuentro, un momento, un arte...* All these definitions naturally said more about the person who conveyed them than about life itself.

Paris, at a chic restaurant near rue Fragonard, a couple is sitting next to our table. I admire the woman's necklace. It is a little cream-coloured enamel tortoise, and we get talking. I tell her what a sweet necklace she is wearing, what a delicate item of jewellery it is. It looks like a real tortoise, I say. *"Vraiment?"* she asks smiling and then removes the necklace, handing it to me. I take it and hold it up to see it better. The tortoise is striking, with such gentle eyes; it is still warm from the woman's neck, and therefore feels alive. But is it only to be admired? I stretch my hand to give it back, and the woman refuses to take it. *"Ça c'est pour moi?"* I ask, to which she nods. I am astonished, speechless. What am I to do faced with such generosity? I have never met the woman before and most probably will never meet her again. I accept graciously, but I need to give something back. Perhaps we should pay for their dinner, or even invite them to London for a weekend and drive them to all the sights. If shown generosity, I need to show generosity tenfold. I finally come to my senses and dare to ask myself whether I would be giving more than the tortoise is worth, though I was brought up to strictly avoid comparing what you receive and what you give. But still, there has to be a fair solution. Like for like. And so, I hand the woman the pink pearl bracelet that I am wearing on my right wrist. It is not a matter of which of the two items is dearer or prettier. It simply boils down to an exchange between two women. There must have been thousands of similar situations going back centuries when people exchanged objects, for gain or no gain. Bartering before money ever arrived and giving things away because possessiveness is not essential for this very short life we live. And back in the Parisian restaurant, both the French woman and I looked at our gifts with pride, but there was a stark difference between us. She placed my bracelet on her wrist, and I put her necklace inside my bag and sort of hid it away. I must confess that I did not really feel attached to the pearl bracelet. I had several of them, in various colours, and it was nothing so important that I could not part away with it readily. My generosity had much less merit than the woman's for sure. As expected, I never saw the woman again, but I still have the necklace. Yet I cannot bring myself to wear it, for I feel that it still belongs to her. It is kept in a box at the very back of one of my drawers, but I can give it to you, if you wish; rest assured that I will not ask for anything in exchange.

I finally realised that 'I shall live' is not the same as 'I don't want to die'.

Memoirs are a blend of the historical truth and the narrative truth; most of the time they coincide, but sometimes storytelling takes over.

Grandmother, in the prim days of the early 20th century, would sew a couple of dry chickpeas on either side of her chemise to insinuate permanently aroused nipples. In those days, it was all about dreaming without touching.

"Se puede pecar de pensamiento, palabra, obra u omisión": as a child, I would try to come up with examples of all these different types of sins, because none of them were clear in my mind. In a way, this religious mandate included all actions, because anything and everything could be considered a sin. Strictly speaking, sins go through a series of stages, all of them corrupt in one way or another: from thinking about an evil act, to mentioning it, to acting it out; or perhaps not doing what you should be doing, and this would be sinning by omission, which is equally contemptible. Thus, we were told, you are born a sinner and you will continue sinning throughout. It is indeed a life of sin, we were reminded. Thus, we were terrified of doing anything in case we sinned; ultimately, we were terrified of life itself.

I repeat: sometimes I talk about myself as *I*, and at other times I talk about myself sometimes as *she*.

He arrived with a bouquet of roses to the divorce lawyer's office and handed them to me. And as we sat down to discuss the final arrangements, the white petals began to fall ever so gently on my lap.

I somehow made it, and this was to be the rule: I did it, coped, endured. Yes, I survived, despite the odds.

Father adored musicals, and at home we had LPs of many famous recordings. As children, we would sing songs from

'My Fair Lady' and suitably dance all along our very large sitting-room. This was to be one of my happiest childhood memories. But what I did not know then was that, as an adult, I would play the role of Pygmalion with several individuals who needed a high degree of constant encouragement, reassurance, and material support, all of it done with my solicitude and to my detriment.

Just a warning: most of all, she is a political animal and, in case you have not noticed, everything she says or does is either extremely political or politically extreme.

Please let me speak before it is all over.

She finally set out to become the introvert she is, without regret or remorse. Until then she had disregarded her feelings of loneliness when in company (and when in a large group, she was very much a woman alone). She forced herself to make an appearance and tried to join in the fun, and everyone thanked her for it without understanding how agonising to the core it was for her. "Did you enjoy yourself?" was the question put to her by all those extroverts, and she smiled gently to make them feel good about themselves.

The little girl I used to be: I am wearing embroidered gloves, pink socks and an impeccable cream organza dress hand-made by Mother, in my right hand a diminutive white handbag shaped like a cylinder. Yes, a perfect creation; something to show your success as a woman, because your brilliant professional career had been ruined by the dictatorship, dear Mother, had it not.

She behaved so very much better than was strictly necessary and did so much more than was commonly required. All of this was her downfall.

During the war, Grandfather walked to a farm that was over five kilometres north of Barcelona. A friend had told him about the availability of a few sacks of potatoes there, but it was more a rumour. Grandfather took a chance and travelled valiantly by foot all the way there, without knowing whether he would find potatoes or perhaps only death. When he arrived home late at night with a few spuds in a bag, all the excited members of the family helped with the peeling. They cut the potatoes in strips and fried them with great care, watching over them in awe as they turned from creamy coloured to light brown. The previous day they had managed to get a cup of unrefined vegetable oil, and so the result was heavenly. They ate those chips slowly and carefully, savouring each morsel for minutes at a time; but the feast was not enough for a family meal. After finishing the last chip, they looked at each other without saying anything, still so very hungry. And Mother –then a young girl– got up and went back to the kitchen to recover the potato peels from the bin and washed them carefully and fried them. The process was repeated all over again, but this time they wept silently with every little morsel.

Father was far too young in a country erratically divided in two, the illuminated and the dark; or technically put, the lawful Republic and a lawless uprising. If you happened to live where the fascists had a stronghold, you were stuck with them unless you wanted to die at dawn. That is how civil wars work.

It was a near-death experience, or more likely an actual death experience. It happened when I heard the doctors say that it was a shame that I had died on the operating table, such a young girl, and that I seemed alert enough when they spoke to me before the operation despite the pain I was suffering, and that I probably had a bright future ahead of me. The diagnosis was a burst appendix, peritonitis, gangrene, death, necessarily in that order. To make matters worse, I was also suffering from bronchitis, as I was a heavy smoker at the time. I heard every word they said as I was lying on the operating table despite being knocked out by the anaesthetic, with the disease-ridden insides of my abdomen exposed to the world. And I thought hard and fast. "Wait a minute; I do not want to die, I screamed, no way, I am nineteen years old, and I have so many plans for my life!" The surgeons paid no attention whatsoever to what I said and went on lamenting the failed operation, as if they were more concerned about their success rate in performing gastrointestinal surgery. I shouted as loud as I could and tried to alert them with my furious hands, to no avail. It was all very much in my distorted mind. And then I saw it: the brightest light above me, as if leading the way, a shining star that lit but did not burn. I will not go away, I said, screaming without being heard and punching the air without moving an inch. I went on shouting at the top of my voice, protesting and fighting back; it seemed like an eternity. My forceful refusal was too much for whoever wanted to take me away, and the bright light began to fade. The next thing I remember was waking up in a hospital room, unsure of whether I was dead or alive. Either the doctors had managed to resuscitate me in the end, or I had been spared because I so very categorically refused to leave this Earth. You can get to choose which of the two accounts you like best.

All those 8mm films from childhood show me primed and moulded into this charming, obedient, wholesome, impeccable little girl who had no say whatsoever in her life. Yes, even then they were intent on making me into the perfectly subdued woman.

It was as if I needed to come out as a writer. Writing became a secret, a no-go area, an unspoken and unproven hypothesis. No friends outside my closely-knit writing circles, and certainly no family member, would ever ask things like how is your writing going, what are you writing about now, how difficult is it to manage writing and all the other stuff that you have to deal with so as to stay alive, and so on. No one seemed interested in the fact that, putting it a tad dramatically, my heart burned with a desire like no other when it came to writing. More importantly, no one knew that my mind perceived the world only in terms of a story: those around me became characters in a play; circumstances I viewed solely as scenes; conversations I likened to potential dialogues. That is how it was: no one asked and, worse still, no one understood. Or if they did ask, which seldom happened, their only question was "*Are you still writing*?" as if there was an alternative.

The most endearing memory I have of Father is of him going around the house switching the lights off and picking up bits of fluff from the floor so that there would be no need to vacuum them. He was a committed environmentalist well before his time.

She speaks two languages, not one after the other, not side by side, not one on Mondays and the other on Tuesdays, but by code-switching constantly: And so here I was telling *a mí misma que no hay nada que* you can learn that does not require *sacrificio y entereza, y que por eso* people are reluctant to take on board *cualquier cosa que les exija dar más de lo que saben or tienen o quieren* as if that were the ultimate proof *para confirmar que su vida es dura, y no la de los demás,* who have it as easy as pie compared to *lo que nosotros somos y aspiramos a ser, y así cambiar* from one language to another at the drop of a hat is the ultimate proof of what we mean to say, *la prueba irrebatible de que queremos mantener nuestra identidad,* albeit divided, *aunque vayamos a contrapelo y no queramos seguir la pista trazada de antemano y así confirmar* that no one can take away from us *lo que es nuestro, por más extraño y difícil que parezca* and as implausible as the principle may be...

In Earls Court, a man in a jogging suit stops alongside me in the street and asks: "How much?" It is 5.55pm, and I am there to collect my daughter from a birthday party at a house in the next street. I am waiting for it to be six o'clock, which is collection time. I should have whacked the man. I should have screamed. I should have called the police. Or perhaps I should have given the man a price beyond his reach.

That spring we were presented with a tiny little goose. In no time at all it became enormous, and with its huge wingspan it would shield my brother and I from the pecking hens in our garden. How much we loved *Gansito*, and how little did we suspect that our parents would betray that love.

This is how it happened at my little school in the outskirts of Madrid: I was late, and when I arrived all my classmates and my teacher had left for an outing. The nature trip was to be a long walk along the meadows and woods nearby. It was a very warm day, so instead of returning home, I set out on my own. Aged six, I walked along fields for what seemed to me like a very long time. My attempt to find my schoolfriends and my teacher proved to be in vain, and I eventually decided to return to school. When I got there, they had already arrived, and my teacher was in shock when I told her that I had been looking for them all over and that I was very excited because it was my first real adventure. And I also told my teacher that, along the route, I met a shepherd and his sheep, a man on a bicycle, a woman carrying a basket of apples on her head, and several stray dogs. And that I heard a distant tune. No, nothing terrible whatsoever happened to me, perhaps it was a very different era. What I did not realise at the time was that my little adventure could perhaps one day become a way of life: travelling on one's own along unknown routes, gazing in awe at the landscape, saying hello to whoever came your way, not having to communicate your thoughts but simply taking it all in, being but a joyful observer of events.

When meeting visitors at home, I was taught by Mother to curtsy and softly smile, ask the visitors how they were and whether they would like me to play a little tune on the piano; and then I would exit the sitting-room, curtsying once again, and go back to my room and play silently with my toys until the visitors left.

Are you happy, I am asked on many occasions by many different people. I suppose it is easier to say *yes* than to explain why I am unhappy.

Father is posted to a mysterious land called England, and we leave our country and embark on an unknown journey from which, especially for the mind, there will be no return.

A WOMAN ALONE

I was but a promise of things to come, yet the main architect of this project was Mother, and she would not live to see whether I had fulfilled that promise. Did I become what Mother would have wished, or even what she would have craved for her own life? I suppose most children ask that question without expecting, or even wanting, an answer.

You look back and see all those decades trickle away like sand. And then someone whispers in your ear: "It is not that those decades did not happen, it is that they were mostly unlived."

My first experience with pain happens when I pick up a burning tin in our garden. Someone has probably thrown it there from a bonfire next-door, whether accidentally or intending to cause damage in a garden with very young children. Interestingly the image of an empty tin persists more than the memory of the pain I suffered. For some reason, I was strangely attracted to the burning tin, a peculiar object lying on the grass, almost red from the heat. I was aged four, but it would not to be the last time I played with fire.

Who is she: too Spanish to be British, too British to be Spanish.

After Mother dies, it is in everyone's best interest that Father remarries as soon as possible. He desperately needs a woman, someone firmly entrenched in the real world and nothing like the ethereal angels he thinks women are.

I leave the bedroom and lock myself in the loo, and such are my sexual experiences for the day.

Yes, my home in Madrid is so very different from other girls' homes. *"¡Tu casa parece un museo!"* one of my schoolfriends says every time she comes over. Other friends even suggest that visiting me feels like stepping into a different era. Yes, home is indeed filled with dark and intricate Chinese antiques and rare Victorian objects, but I now think that my friends were referring more to the inhabitants than to the things on display.

Being a woman is not that difficult –anyone can be a woman, for there are many ways of being one. It is a role that can be learnt all the way to its last detail. What is difficult is to live, in any condition, under any guise, in any circumstance, with any gender.

"El cielo y el infierno están en esta tierra" as Grandfather used to say after every single incident, whether good or bad.

Just before attending mass with my family at the Almudena Cathedral in Madrid, we find a tiny kitten in the Sabatini Gardens, beside the Royal Palace, and I hide her in my little cylindrical handbag. I am, what, three and a bit probably. There and then I name her Saba, after the architect who had designed those lovely gardens. During mass at the cathedral, Saba begins to meow in desperation. In my most soothing childish voice, I whisper to her to be quiet, and strangely she obeys at once. She is already as discreet as everyone at home is expected to be at all times, meowing just to herself.

There really is nothing to knowing other languages. You just need to have a wider vocabulary and a marginally more complex set of emotions.

I am in hospital for a whole month after my appendicitis and peritonitis operation, and the woman Father is set to marry stays with me in my hospital room every single night. Under literally the pain of death, I am not allowed to eat or drink, and every hour she will soak a handkerchief in fresh water and run it through my very dry mouth so that I can get some relief from my abysmal thirst. It is the kind of selfless act that will never be forgotten.

As an autobiographer she does not necessarily know more on the subject than anyone else.

A little girl is crossing the road. It is me, yes, it is me! Look at her, so credulous and playful, so much in awe of everything around her. My uniform is green, the colour of Concorde pears. The beret has a pompom, the colour of egg yolk. I am the girl who has just arrived in this new country and who barely speaks this new language. She does not comprehend one bit what is going on around her and is striving to make some sense of it all. When people speak to me, I have been taught what to say, at least phonetically: "I doooh nooohhhttt aaaoonndeehstaaand Eeengleeesh!" That is what the little girl replies when anyone asks her anything, whatever it may be: the time, directions, whether she would like a cup of tea. She uses the same reply with all her new schoolmates and teachers, for she was told not to talk to strangers, something that was never mentioned back home – back home you spoke to everyone, and everyone spoke to you, and you could even walk on your own along fields and meadows and then return safely back home. She was only then beginning to understand the country of her birth, and now she has been taken away and is here in this new and strange land, feeling completely at a loss. There is no going back, someone says in her head. Around her all these extraneous voices and shrills, unfamiliar sayings, peculiar habits, trials every step of the way. In the first few weeks, she has managed to memorise a few words of that new language. She knows the world *girl* from before, as this was her very first word, but now she can make a whole sentence about homework, the weather, the route to school. I must learn all these new things as fast as I can: the language, the customs, the gestures, the idioms, the culture, the appropriateness of what I must do and say at any given time. She repeats all this to herself every morning before going to school. I should speak and think and behave just like they do. In fact, even better than they do. They must believe, and soon, that I am one of them. And I must believe, deep down, that I am one of them too.

If I stop, it will be the end of me.

Oh, the feeling of doing nothing whatsoever, allowing time to trickle by without a care in the world and wasting it entirely when we could be using it for something important. *"¡No pierdas el tiempo!"* Mother used to say repeatedly. And whatever I was doing, even when frightfully busy with serious matters like homework or with basic chores like tidying up my room, I always thought that I was wasting my time and that I ought to be using it even more wisely. And after all these years and the many recriminations, it turns out that doing nothing at all, even staring at a blank wall, might be the most useful thing I can do for my sanity.

Father always said to me: *"El inglés te salvará."* I never knew whether he was he referring to the English language or to an Englishman.

To speak a new language demands, among other things, matching words and experiences. However, in your new language there may be no words for certain experiences you had in the past; likewise, you will learn words in your new language for which you have not yet acquired the experiences to match. And this collection of voids, where words and experiences are not yet adequately tallied, will also need to be very carefully stage-managed alongside any languages you may speak. Ultimately, the combination of all these words and voids will eventually become a private dialect of some sort. If you are really lucky, you might be able to find someone with whom you can speak in that particular dialect and accurately communicate without any outsiders understanding either of you. Meeting someone like that is, as might be expected, a chance in at least a million.

Imposing my tastes: If you have not watched Cimino's 'Heaven's Gate', then you have watched no film whatsoever. If you have not heard bass László Polgár as Prince Gremin, then you have heard no music whatsoever. If you have not seen '*El Transparente*' in Toledo's Cathedral, then you do not know what ecstasy is. And if you have not spent a night in a Kasbah, then you have not yet experienced what the brightest stellar skies can do to you.

She is not asked to join in the family photographs; after all, she is not an official member of the family. Do not take a single picture of her, they say, because she will be dropped as yet another of the many girlfriends who were soon dropped and forgotten.

On the word *patronage*: There is such a thing as supporting authors via a website that turns you into literally a patron.

Perhaps I should look for patrons and finally start making dosh from my writing. Yet how can a writer ask other writers for money; we are not benefactors of the arts, and so patronage should be something that only the rich do to make them feel better, as if they are contributing to the progress of this Earth by supporting impoverished artists. But patronage should never come from the artists themselves; they are far too busy making art to be making money.

From my much-loved anthem: "I was lost, but now I am found."

On the most tedious wall in my house, with no paintings or prints or tapestries or embroidered silk, there appears a bright rainbow strip that –when the light is just right– shines all the way from an upstairs window. Is the explanation to be found solely in Physics?

... my children were my teachers were my children were my teachers were my children...

I am given general guidelines by medics, but I make up my own exercises, verbal and physical. To recover my speech, which has been mildly affected, I invent various absurd words to say at increasing speed, like *pripriprá, gloglogró, mumutrú, dedresé* and the like. And to fully recover the somewhat impaired movement on my right side, from head to toe, I begin to gradually move, and later on shake, twirl, skip, bounce, hop and dance. As to the damage done to the mind, that is a little more demanding, and I am still trying to come to a truce with myself.

They all tell you what to do in no uncertain terms: one tried to get me to like Radiohead; another tried to get me to eat meat; and another tried to get me to categorically love all the members of his family, that is, to blindly accept any misdemeanour whatsoever from them.

Father and Mother were both exceedingly law-abiding, except that on one or two occasions they carried alcohol in the car when crossing the border. One day a customs officer enquired about them carrying liquor in the car, and my parents vehemently denied it. And me, being the truthful child that I was, said in a loud voice to my parents' disbelief: *"But, sir, we do have wine bottles hidden in the boot of the car."* And I would have continue confessing, if asked: but I have seen my parents spit in the street; but they sometimes shout horribly at each other; but we are not really that well off. If you are an adult, the truth sucks.

Believe it or not, the last thing I want to do here is to talk about myself, for I am the most ardent recluse.

In hospital, they have a large circular chamber with several coffins placed centrally, all in a radius-like position like the hours on a clock; the coffins are surrounded by small areas for mourners and are separated from such areas by glass screens. Each coffin is somewhat tilted as if a box of chocolates on the shop window of a *patisserie*. The place is so well designed (much like a panopticon) that a nurse can, in one sweep, make sure that the dead are at the appropriate angle for disconsolate relatives to suitably say their farewells and not grieve the wrong corpse instead. From where I am, the only visible features of Mother are a rigid forehead and firmly shut eyes. Her head is covered with a shroud doubling up as a tight headscarf holding together her deconstructed jaw, a non-fatal yet unsightly corollary of her illness. One of the nurses comes over to Mother's coffin and gently touches her covered head, as if confirming that she is well and truly lifeless. And then the nurse smiles ever so briefly in my direction, standing as I am behind the screen and weeping silently, something which a teenager finds very hard to do.

Even to remove cobwebs, she needs to dress up as a warrior.

There are three buttresses that are still holding me together to this day, despite all the setbacks and upheavals: to dispel darkness, clarity; to dismiss ignorance, alertness; to soothe agitation, equanimity.

She even invented stories for those around her and would reproach them for being such lousy actors and for not remembering the lines she had written especially for them.

When we return to live in Spain, I tell Mother that I miss speaking English and that Spanish is far too difficult for me. For a while I even refuse to speak Spanish, not that my Spanish is any good. I find Spanish verbs to be particularly challenging. Without saying a word, Mother sits at her desk and for an hour or so she is seen writing something very intricate on a large piece of paper. What she prepares I can only describe as the most complex diagram I ever saw. It is a large hand-written sheet with all the verbal modes and tenses of a regular verb, definitely from the first conjugation; Mother obviously starts with the simple before moving to the highly complex. I look at Mother's spidery writing covering most of the page and am amazed that she knows all this. To my shock, she tells me to quickly learn by heart all that very complicated material. I have two choices, despair and give up; or do as Mother says, learn and memorise. I sit down patiently trying to untangle, first, her writing, and then, the intricacies of but one verbal conjugation. When after much patience and dedication I learn all that information by heart –at first not understanding a word but eventually coming to grips with it and even beginning to enjoy it– I realise that there are other conjugations, second and third, plus irregular verbs, plus ever so many exceptions to the rules, plus other issues that I did not even suspect existed in the world of language. It is intriguing how some life-long passions come into existence.

I am at the outskirts of Madrid, waiting on my own in a large room full of empty chairs, and then I am led along this impossibly dark corridor (could it be the garden path, I begin to wonder). A door opens into an office almost as dark, with three men inside. They are all dressed in grey suits as befits TV executives in that decade and in most decades. It is summertime and I am wearing a thin pink dress. The temperature outside is 35 degrees centigrade. I tell them I would like to work as an intern over the summer, before my next term starts. What else is there to say? Inside my shoulder bag I have my CV ready, notes from my university lectures, pieces of writing that were published, a poem or two. The three men look at each other, then examine me carefully. They smile, one even shakes his head from side to side. They ask only one thing: *"¿Por cuántas manos estás dispuesta a pasar?"* I cannot understand the question. I translate this into English in my mind, for I cannot believe what I am hearing. How many men are you willing to lie with? On my part, I continue thinking and reasoning in English throughout the episode, for it is still very much my main language. Can you repeat your question, I request, because I am under the impression that they said something that they did not really mean. And one of them utters exactly the same question, emphasising the key words or at least that is how I hear the question in my mind: "How many MEN are YOU willing to LIE with?" You mean, I begin to say but cannot finish the sentence. Yes, they reply, exactly that. Is it lie as in lie, or lie as in lie? Are they referring to deceit or to sexual encounters? I somehow suspect they are resorting to the archaic use of the English word because speaking openly and directly might embarrass them, the dears. I look at them, as insatiable and suntanned as they are. I get up and start walking in the direction of the exit and take my leave without saying goodbye. I cannot deal with the situation, and I have to get away as soon as possible, in those days this wanting to flee happens to me regularly. I then hear merriment behind me, but I do not look back until I leave the building, trying to put it all behind me. Outside I realise I have just missed the bus. The sign says that there are no more buses for several hours. I will scream, or maybe I will jump onto the oncoming traffic. No, screaming is not the right thing to do, and jumping in front of cars will never solve this. Right now, I have to get home, and later I will think about what to do about what has just happened. I have plenty of time; I mean, the city is ten kilometres away. A train station in the proximity will not be built until 2007. I decide to walk. I am now walking at my fastest pace alongside the main road. Endless cars are travelling in both directions. A man stops his Renault and I get in. Stupid girl, I blame myself. Whether it is because I did not scream at the TV executives or because I got into a stranger's car is anyone's guess. *"¿A Madrid?"* he asks. *"Sí"* I reply. Half a mile down the road, the man stops the car in readiness to take a turning. I look up and there is a narrow side road leading to a hill where grows a very tall tree. It must be a great vantage point from which to admire the city. But I see it as a verdant resting place, with my name etched on a memorial plaque and flowers placed by my family, year after year, on the anniversary of my death resulting from rape and asphyxiation. *"¿Ahí?"* I ask. The man grins but does not reply to my question. I now have a good look. He is so much older than Father. He has a moustache the colour of dust, and his eyes flicker like a butterfly. His hands are trembling around the wheel, waiting as he is for a gap in the traffic in order to turn into the side road. And risking all, as the car starts to move I open the door and jump out. Onto the road I fall. I am grazed more than injured, hurting my legs and arms. The car travelling behind us just misses me. Get back in the car, I think the man shouts. Go away or I will call the police, I think I say. But where can I phone from, how. There are no phone boxes nearby, mobiles have yet to be invented. The police will claim that it serves me right. It is all your fault for getting into a stranger's car, is it not, I can hear them say. It was all her fault, will be the narrative for a very long time in such cases. And as I am thinking all these things, the man pulls towards him the open door on the passenger side to lock it and drives off in a huff. What am I to do, in the middle of nowhere, it will be dark by the time I get to the nearest station; no trains will be running by then. I have no option but to stick my thumb out and stop a car along the main road. As expected, I am tearful, despairing. Another Renault stops, with three young men inside. I now have three more chances of getting raped and being murdered. But I am proved wrong. They are students, inexperienced and unworldly, yet entirely trustworthy. They ask me why I am there, in the middle of the road, hitchhiking, crying, hurt. I tell them about the man who gave me a lift, and how I had to throw myself from his car onto the road. They say that they are ashamed about one of their kind. I also tell them about the three executives, my request for an internship, my rushing out of the TV studios in shock. They seem even more ashamed, as if responsible for other men's misdemeanours. What I have just experienced is hardly a worst-case scenario, I reply to them, it could have all been so much more vicious. Should I then keep quiet about what has taken place and tell no one apart from the three students, I ask myself in the meantime. If I do nothing about today's events, I could be held responsible for what happens to others in the future. And yet I do keep quiet, much saddened and distraught. But I will not stay quiet for long.

This was a difficult section to write. I could not put the idea precisely into words, probably because it is a complex idea: the feeling of familiarity when things go wrong, the sense of death about to arrive and of things constantly ending, the certainty that love and life are being sucked out of you on a daily basis. As if desolation were the default, and joyful moments were nothing but exceptions. Having written this, it is not exactly what I wanted to say, but almost there. This is the proof, then, that ideas come first, and we try shoehorning them into our human speech without much luck or enthusiasm or accuracy.

Who says that I cannot do this? Is it you by any chance?

After the war, Grandmother opened a tiny haberdashery in a street in central Barcelona, and it became a very popular establishment. Apart from sewing implements and threads of many colours, she also sold home-made costume jewellery. Items of jewellery were created with small wooden mounts made by Grandfather in his workshop and decorated with tiny flowers moulded from flour and dyed in various colours by Mother and her two siblings. Grandmother went from being a grand lady to being the funniest and friendliest shopkeeper in the area. People would flock to her little shop more to have a conversation with her than to buy her colourful merchandise.

A WOMAN ALONE

One of my stories about the subject of murder is called *'Cómo cometer un asesinato sin tener que mover un dedo'*, and it begins like this: *Para matar a alguien lo mejor es saber dónde vive. Conviene tener los detalles del domicilio: el país, la ciudad, el barrio, la calle, el número del portal, el piso. Si la escalera es la de la izquierda o la de la derecha. Si la letra de la puerta –la A, la B, la C o la D– es la correcta. Y sobre todo si el interesado no sospecha el mal rato que vamos a hacerle pasar. Pese a todo, habría que andarse con cuidado porque en ese mismo edificio puede haber otros que guarden cierto parecido con nuestra potencial víctima pero que no se merecen tanto, o incluso otros que puede que se lo merezcan más. Hasta otros que nos lo agradecerían con efusividad si lográramos fulminarlos para siempre de la faz del planeta, pues así les evitaríamos la considerable molestia de tener que hacerlo ellos por su cuenta. Pero no estamos aquí para hacer favores a nadie. Si estamos aquí es para impartir justicia a un hombre por la violación que cometió hace ya veinte años...*

I am left alone at home with my new-born child for a couple of hours. I am out-and-out shattered after a very lengthy, painful, and complicated birth. Sent home from hospital because I had not dilated enough, waters breaking, long hours of pain, back in hospital, again not enough dilation, an epidural administered, foetal distress, the umbilical cord around the baby's neck, all my alarming panting and pushing, the colossal episiotomy. Finally, back at home I find breastfeeding intolerably draining, as if I am feeding my child with the last remnants of my soul. And I sit on an armchair with the baby on top of my belly, both of us crying helplessly; I cannot bring myself to move an inch, unable to comfort her or myself. And there we both are: squealing and howling, a new-born girl who understands nothing of the world she has been thrust to without having asked for it; and a new mother who has no idea of what she got herself into by giving birth. And then I say the words, strange words for a non-believer: "Please Lord, take me away!"

There came a time when every single day was catastrophic. I took minor things so very badly: making a phone call, sending an email, enjoying a joke.

Grandfather invented 3-D photography, but only he and the family knew about his invention. He did not wish to divulge it and, for a very long time indeed, he kept it to himself as a pastime (another introvert who suffered greatly because of his dammed discretion). And when he decided that he would finally announce his revolutionary creation to the world, it was far too late because it had already been invented and launched and commercialised and exploited, even surpassing his own version in both quality and, chiefly, quantity.

You may be sitting comfortably and reading all these things, but do not forget that I am going through hell to narrate them to you.

Fragments from the beginning of Father's memoir: *"Ésta es la historia de mi vida de soldado, que puede estar escrita con cierta visión infantil de las cosas, ya que vi el cuartel por primera como vio Alicia las piezas de ajedrez dentro del mundo al revés del espejo, todas de una misma madera, con papeles diferentes, y cuando se me dijo que allí unos entraban por la puerta grande y otros por la puerta de servicio, creí que aquello era como la casa del hombre que tenía dos gatos, uno grande y otro pequeño, y para que entrasen y saliesen hizo en la puerta un agujero grande y otro pequeño, el uno para el gato grande y el otro para el gato pequeño..."*

A dream about a wall and a precipice: I am walking on top of a rather wide wall; on one side there is a precipice and on the other are endless overgrown shrubs, under which there could well be another precipice. From where I am, I can see the bluest ocean. I keep walking along the wall just to get there, but when I look again there is only a vast stretch of land fading into the horizon and no sign of any sea or body of water. Continuing the journey is fraught with danger, with a precipice on one side and a likely precipice on the other; what is worse is that the wall seems to be getting narrower by the minute. I stop and think: the wisest thing to do is to go back. And despite all the signs telling me to return, I am undecided as to what to do, still on top of the narrowing wall, looking towards that inexistent sea, trying to forget the place I came from.

The usual contradictions: she is a fiercely private person, but then those who write for a living need an audience as a matter of life and death.

When returning from London to Madrid as an adolescent, I suffered chaotic and contradictory sensations for a long while: surfaces that were rough and smooth at the same time, a kind of sensory oxymoron; I heard voices telling me sarcastically that I could do things so well, so very well, so exceedingly well, hahaha; and when it came to understanding what was being said, it was not so much about the language used but about the perplexing people themselves. So much was at stake: my two countries, my two languages, my two *personas*.

Women's history is mostly an oral history, and our knowledge was passed from generation to generation by word of mouth through traditions and rituals: from dialogues that held many of the secrets of civilization and progress over centuries to the teachings of universal folklore and mythologies. It is a history that still needs to be fully and painstakingly documented. Until then, we must write it down individually, one by one.

My Great-grandfather died in the War of Cuba in 1898. At the time, his wife was pregnant with his son, my beloved Grandfather. I still have my Great-grandfather's last letter, sent from Havana, with extraordinarily slanted writing on a sheet of paper that has become ochre with time. The letter includes the outline of the machete he was attacked with and which the attacker left behind. The story goes that the aggressors returned the next day, bringing with them an even larger machete, this time with fatal consequences; you would have needed a broadsheet to draw the outline of that second weapon. Putting an end to imperialism may require several attempts; in some cases when one imperialist power is finally defeated another one takes over.

Femininity was firmly demanded in those days, not just as a mandatory feature in females but more as an ultimatum.

To my parents I was supposedly a disappointment for being a girl and not a first-born son (and thus I always had to excel myself in everything I did to make them like me, at least this was my interpretation), but to my maternal grandparents I, as the first born of all their grandchildren, became their favourite, the shiniest apple of their eye. As expected, my grandparents were the ones I most loved in the family and, especially, the ones I most learnt from as I was so lovingly receptive to their ideas.

Someone who is gaslighting you will deny things that are unashamedly true, make you question your memories and loyalties, weaponise your displays of emotion against you. He very clearly said to me: "Who would want to have a relationship with a divorced woman with two kids? I do, so you have to be eternally grateful towards me and pay through the nose."

I was collecting my child from a house in Eaton Square. She had been playing with her wealthy friend, and I needed to collect her at 6pm on the dot, but I was 45 minutes late. Because of traffic, I replied to the uniformed maid who opened the door. Under the marble staircase of this most glorious property, she made me sit on a chair designed more for dropping bags than for accommodating humans. From where I was, I could see a large room full of guests. There was a party going on for the adults on the ground floor whilst the children were upstairs, out of sight and definitely out of mind. At first, I thought that the party was a fancy-dress event, for I had never seen clothes as gleaming and exquisite. But clothes seemed to be the only thing differentiating them, since all those adults were very much alike: well-fed but so skinny and taut the women; well-sculpted but so overweight and overbearing the men. Some of them looked towards me from afar and spoke among themselves. The hostess eventually came to where I was sitting and nodded to me by way of hello, and then went back to her guests. I was not offered champagne as the guests were having, but only told by the maid to wait until my child was brought down to the ground floor. The value, if any, of money shapes some and hideously distorts others.

Tell them what you would not even tell a shrink, she very strongly suggested when I mentioned that I was writing this memoir.

"*Cristo reina*" – this is the sentence you would use to greet to a nun from school if you happened to meet her in the street, and she would reply: "*Por siempre en nuestros corazones.*" I could not understand, for my Spanish was not that good then, why the female of *rey* was used to describe a male, but I dared not ask. It was only when I further got the hang of verbs that I realised that in this case *reina* was from the verb *reinar*, to reign. And even when I understood that the sentence meant "He forever reigns in our hearts" I still could not categorically comprehend what this meant.

In those days the only way to grieve was to wake up the next day and get on with your life.

He asked me to lift my right leg and place it on a stool, all very calculated and calm; and then he performed some kind of sub-standard *cunnilingus*, all very premeditated and composed. He was more inexperienced than youthful. I was more polite than cynical. Without a prelude, the composition fell flat on its nose.

Such different schooling in the two countries: analyse and discuss (*explorar*) versus memorise and repeat (*empollar*). Dialogue versus enforcement of what they claimed was knowledge. Discerning the truth versus believing without proof. Facts over fabrications. Mind over clutter.

You must call her mother because you don't have a mother, he said. Naturally I have a mother, I didn't just happen to sprout from a tree or a stone; I was most definitely born from a woman; and she is the only one who can be called mother by me; and if she is no longer alive, I will call no one else mother. You are wrong, he said, you must call her by that name, mother. He would always say that when confronted: *you are wrong*. And what can you reply to that sort of statement except with the words: *I am right*.

Cases of corruption in the workplace? Oh, so very common. I was a witness of innumerable incidents. I even paid the price of their corruption for I was on the receiving end of injustice and transgressions on several occasions. No names given, only initials. I bet I could use all the letters of the alphabet several times over both for the perpetrators and their crimes.

A few years later, my parents tried their luck again, and it was another girl. But on this occasion, she was welcomed with open arms. Oh, there was so much joy when she was born. No intimations at all from my parents that they would next try for a boy. She was a bright and beautiful and bouncy baby sister. With a decade between us, we were so much alike in both body and mind. Just like true soulmates.

Water: I seem to get my best ideas when the precious liquid is around: whether swimming in the sea, or on a boat gliding across a river, or in the bathtub, or even drinking a long and cool glass of water on the rocks with something interesting added.

Mother's best friends were Ursula, from Bonn, and Marguerite, from Paris. How they met I do not know, and I would need to do more research on the subject. Once or twice, I overheard curious things about them at home, and in my young and inventive mind I always suspected that cold war politics or even espionage were the explanation for these friendships. So, I made up suitably entertaining stories about those two women as being hardened spies. What I did know for sure was that all three of them, Ursula and Marguerite and Mother, met in Spain after the second World War. Ursula was a tall and sophisticated woman, and she would visit Madrid on a regular basis, most probably representing her parents' toy factories –this is why most of my toys were German and I was brought up reading the adventures of mischievous *"Max und Moritz"* without really knowing the language; my sweet boy-doll (which I still have, sitting here beside me) was called Günther; and the little hedgehogs and wood animals dressed in fine clothing I played with were all manufactured in Germany. As to Marguerite, I remember well her warm smile, and especially the fact that she would always bring me bergamot sweets when she visited; but I cannot remember her profession, if I was ever told. One interesting detail about her: she loved citrus smells, and apparently before leaving the house she would always squirt a tangerine segment on her neck. After all these years, I suppose leaving behind little dolls or trails of scent were not clever things to do if they had really been spies.

All those relatives who came to stay with us at home for a few months, ended up staying for five solid years. Yes, I can hear you asking: "And how on earth did you survive that sort of thing?" And my reply is: "I didn't!"

I never knew my paternal grandparents –it appears that she had the most beautiful red hair and very sadly died young, and he was as authoritarian as those grim times required. Of him there was an old photograph, now lost, that displayed his stern face with two candles behind him, showing on either side of his head, which gave him a devilish appearance; from her I have a bracelet with rubies, as red as her hair would have been.

As a child, eating meat looked to me like someone had torn a piece of flesh from my arm and had served it to me, agreeably roasted, on a plate. And when you told people that you hated meat and that it felt like you were consuming someone's flesh, you were punished for refusing to eat it. They shouted at you and smacked you, even though you were such a young child. *"¡Cómete la carne!"* they screamed.

There is only one full name that I will provide here: my great-uncle Florencio Brabo was a well-known poet in his time. He was born in Valladolid in mid-19th century, and dedicated his poetry mostly to his wife, who died young. A few years later, he also died when still a young man. His life always reminded me of Manuel Machado, the lesser known of the two Machados. My uncle's books are now totally out of print. Luckily, I still have a copy of one of them; unluckily, it has almost turned into dust.

Tired, you ask. Yes, I am tired. So many responsibilities from a young age: looking after a home and a family while Mother is in hospital; then during her recovery; then while she is again sick; then after she is dead. Going to school, getting the grades, thinking about the future (what future?), going to university; and all that while, working as a language teacher and then as a journalist and a broadcaster and a linguist. And all of this happened well before I entered life as a fully-fledged adult and began my professional life. So there: I am tired, that is all there is to it.

I was brought up to believe that concealing your real age was fundamentally important. It was all about the social conditioning that pervaded those times. Mother even had a reduced age engraved on her tombstone; four years less than her factual age, to be precise. But I think that her reluctance to admit her real age was also Father's fault, after all he was the one who commissioned the inscription on the tombstone; concealing Mother's age also meant concealing his.

My first poetry book was called *'Ciudad del interior'* to reflect the architecture of my dreams: a city with streets and squares and public parks to which I would return every few nights, all of them linked by a complicated underground system where certain tube lines offered no return journeys but led instead to dark and dead and very silent ends.

I was there, a young student surrounded by thousands who cheered and clamoured. Aghast, I looked on, a mere witness to what the media at the time called a truly extraordinary and historic event. Two dictators travelling in an open-topped limousine along the *Gran Vía* (which in those days was called *Avenida del Generalísimo*): Franco and Nixon. One a dictator with several decades of diehard experience, and the other a wannabe dictator, for within two years the Watergate scandal would begin to unravel. Nixon wanted to influence both the present and the future of Spain; affirm the Treaty of Friendship and Cooperation that had just been signed by the two countries; and on the more practical side, make sure that American military bases on Spanish soil would be safe for a long time to come. And all this while, the world was watching and doing very little (as tragically happened at the break of the civil war). Yes, it was the stuff of nightmares, a democracy supporting a fascist dictatorship. I very much admire the opera 'Nixon in China' by John

Adams, and have always wondered whether an opera about Nixon's brief visit to Spain could have been equally exhilarating: with a countertenor in the role, small and chubby in size just like the dictator himself, wearing a flashy olive-green uniform, with dozens of medals and other colourful paraphernalia and looking through very dark glasses, though possibly a castrato voice would be more adequate; and with the equivalent of Madame Mao as the taller and more physically impressive singer, a coloratura soprano with endless strings of pearls dangling haphazardly from her neck. Yes, the dictator had an exceedingly light voice, so much at odds with the gruesome tyrant who governed with an iron-fist and created a terror state, had zero tolerance for any kind of dissent, firmly believed that the civil war had been a crusade, and kept the mummified hand of Saint Teresa encased in silver beside his bed for good luck. As to the opera itself, perhaps in Act 1 the dictator would sing a deeply felt aria that began with the same words he used to open his speeches: *"Españoles todos"*. In Act 2, the dictator would sing about another favourite theme of the regime: *"Cuarenta años de paz."* And in Act 3, his aria would be about *"El complot judeo-masónico"*, blaming the rest of the world for what he thought were dark conspiracies aimed at destabilising the country. Even in his very last speech shortly before his death, the dictator mentioned this once more: *"Todo obedece a una conspiración judeo-masónica-izquierdista."* All these views now seem preposterous and laughable, but at the time such were the watchwords of a brutal and dictatorial regime.

The exact day I reached majority of age I left Father's home –therefore, it all happened on my birthday. I packed my things and left, as simple as that. A small van came over and parked outside the house, and it took me and all my stuff away. It turned out to be a very sad occasion, with every member of the family weeping at my departure, especially my two siblings. I held back my tears, confident that leaving home was the right thing to do. Yet, if I could go back and change just one thing in my life, it would be this one. I should have stayed at Father's home with him and his new wife, and I should have tried my best to live with them despite the difficulties. It is, unquestionably, what a true stoic would have done.

Without moving so much as an inch from the house, she began a long and beguiling journey.

I can see that I am wearing a tie. This little girl always thought that ties were only for men. It may be the school uniform, but this little girl is far too feminine for those things. She has been brought up to be a prim and proper girl, to curtsy on arrival and to wear flimsy dresses and black patent leather shoes with a shiny buckle and pristine white socks. No, she does not get dirty or run or fall on the mud. Above all, her clothes must never be soiled, and her skin must never get a single scratch. And despite the propaganda she is fed daily at home and at school and by the meagre media of the time, she begins to think that the world, the real world out there with sludge and muck, with kids falling and getting hurt, with things going wrong and people being difficult, does not belong to her, and she certainly does not belong to it. She will question all of this later and feel despondent and eventually begin to act more in line with the values she will wish to uphold, but not for a while yet. For now, there are no questions asked, merely inconsistent thoughts. But the seed of doubt has been planted in her mind because, quite simply, such pointless distractions from the fundamental make no sense whatsoever in her mind.

The doctors say that my brain is apparently being remodelled after the ischaemic episodes I suffered, since sections of it literally died during the event. But I would like to know whether I can have a say in the remodelling process and intervene in my capacity as the rightful owner of that ineffable organ so that I do not go back to the old ways of stressing, or become restless at the drop of a hat, or exert myself beyond what is humanly possible. But more importantly, I would like to dispel forever the prevailing feelings of inadequacy and remorse and culpability that have been moulding me all these years.

During childbirth the mid-wife kept telling me not to push now, dear, but when I tell you to, dear, but not yet, dear. But then I pushed when I ought not to, because in those moments of agony you feel like being totally disobedient and doing the opposite of what you are told to do. Strictly speaking, it was an act of insubordination. Yes, I did it all myself, tore my own flesh all the way down to the anal passage. I did not feel a thing then, because what is a tear of the flesh compared to a body expanding beyond what is right and natural, with the birth canal opening from accommodating only a small amount of hardened flesh in the shape of some kind of stake to a large and structured and bony head? At the time the mid-wife told me off, and kept repeating the word *naughty*, but she did not explain that the tear would interfere with my sex life later on. So, when enough time had elapsed for the wound to heal several times over, I went to see a specialist.

I was brought up thinking I should be someone else, as simple as that. Mother kept insisting over and over again that she should have married another man instead of Father. It was the love of her life, she used to say, but at the time her family was less well off than his family, and her confessor persuaded her to steer well away from him. During confession, in that darkest of places and in those even darker times, people could be swayed and their minds changed, particularly the impressionable young. The priest did the same with the guy, the only son of the richest family in the area, driving him away from the most charming girl he had ever met. That confessionary became thus a place where to manipulate the young and uphold the sanctity of landowners. And in the light of such a story as told to me by Mother, these were my thoughts: if Mother had married the man she loved as a teenager, who would I be then? What would I have of what I now have, and what would have been forfeited? I kept asking myself such questions throughout the duration of my childhood. And what is a child supposed to think of herself in such cases: that she is nothing, that she should not exist, that she personifies the fruit of error and penance? And the most important question of all: would Mother have loved me more?

If on a particular night I suffered from insomnia, I would spend it reading pages and pages and pages from 'Bleak House'.

Fairy tales begin with the disruption of family life, and their endings are usually about a return to the original state of harmony. Probably all my attempts at anything had to do with restoring family life, which in my case had been so prematurely shattered. Failed attempts on my part they all were, by the way.

I never thought of her death as a curse or a disappearance, but merely as a straightforward case of abandonment. I suppose this is the reason why, for many years I regularly dreamt that Mother had not died but was instead being treated in a clinic in Switzerland. And in such dreams, Mother phoned us to confirm that she would return home once doctors had given her the thumbs up.

Stuff chronology in memoirs!

A sort of lullaby: both during pregnancy and after birth, I would sing *"Tres morillas"* to my babies.

In a cafeteria in the centre of town, Mother and Father are whispering and swapping niceties. No bodily fluids have been exchanged yet; that will only happen once rings are placed on fingers. Except, of course, for the exchange of air exhaled out of lungs that agonised during the many episodes of the war: the bombing, the shelling, the barraging. He wants her, oh how he wants her, but she is not so sure about wanting him. There are hardly any men left after the conflict, she keeps reminding herself, and to make matters worse we fought on opposing sides; me, the Republican; and he, on the wrong side, for he is the enemy, one of the rebels and insurgents and mutineers. Oh, but there are many ways to talk about the rebellion, he claims, because in his case he had no choice, he keeps reminding her, too young, caught on the wrong side, I would have been shot if I had behaved according to my conscience. Conscience is a word far-removed from a country torn apart, frayed. It is considered too radical to have a conscience; awareness, perhaps; observation, maybe. But not conscience, please. Your conscience, she has asked him so many times, where is it now? He cannot bring himself to provide an answer to that sort of subject, at least for now. Instead, he says: "*¡Eres tan bella!*" His red hair is unusual, with twists and curls and waves; his looks are decidedly foreign, as if from a country yet to be discovered. She suspects that there is no part in his body not covered by freckles, and she smiles to herself. But he will do, because she is almost thirty and counting. As things are in the present situation, she thinks, no woman is complete without marriage; if unmarried, she will have failed; will not be taken seriously; her destiny unfulfilled; her life wholly pointless. Conventions are as entrenched as the enemy; traditions can be as deadly as firepower. Oh, but had it been otherwise, with all that social and familial pressure removed, she would have had a shining future in the world of academia. Anything other than being cooped up at home, transferring the reading of Philosophy to the reading of Gastronomy. In his eyes, though, it is not about convenience and customs, but about poetry and ultimately love. For she has the arms that the Venus de Milo would have possessed. Marble-like, sleek, smooth, slight, evanescent. He wants to forget that hunger created those arms. They are the fruit of occasional potato peels, tossed in a little oil and fried, for the three long consecutive years of the war. And still those arms are nothing but a masterpiece, he cannot stop fantasising. Yes, Father and Mother have known each other for only a few weeks, meeting when learning English in some major foreign institution established in the capital (not that the dictatorship has allowed too many of those in the country). He says that progress is in language, freedom is very much in words. And as he utters such things, which she may or may not agree with, he dares to stretch his right hand in her direction, slowly moving across the table, trying not to upset the two coffees and the plate with a small pastry the name of which he has forgotten because he has not tasted one since before the war, and which she is eating in tiny morsels, for her stomach is not yet used to good things after all those years of deprivation, famine, the stench of death and the flavour of gun powder. And his hand, moving as slowly as he would move with his bayonet on the ground to catch the enemy unawares back in the *Ofensiva*, eventually lands on her arm, sculpted by a Greek, lean, delicate, glowing, formed like a column in a temple raised to a goddess in charge of versifying or making love or both. Possibly Grace, possibly Abundance, possibly Discretion. And he strikes up the courage to tell her all those things about her arms (how can he not have the courage after a three-year long agonising conflict, with most men still in their teens). But she, the daughter of a railway man who lost his fortune when business went sour and war turned out to be a way of life, is not used to such niceties, because after the war came the consequences of the war, in many ways so much worse. There has been much forgetting, she thinks; there was no other way of coping but by forgetting. Yes, hunger has made her forget about soft puff pastries; and cruel war dispatches have made her forget about the existence of dreamy words. She still cannot understand why someone should be admiring her skinny arms, so pale from malnutrition. For she, about to be thirty, can only think in practical terms. Marriage, children, even if it costs me my prized job as executive secretary to the director general of one of the largest companies in the city, because yesterday's big companies are today's big companies, such enterprises always impervious to the changes on the political arena, however blood-spattered. And as things are then, a woman who decides to get married will lose her job, for it is assumed that marriage and a professional life are wholly incompatible. And so, in that open-air cafeteria, under the gentle May breeze, the waiter in his bleached and starched jacket, the threadbare bits cleverly concealed with a touch of his wife's transparent nail varnish, comes over to their table and, looking at Father's fingers most gently touching Mother's sculpted arm, tells them, in no uncertain terms, to leave; and then he places the bill on the table. What do you mean? Father asks with his astonished eyes. The waiter looks in the direction of the fingers barely reaching the arm of a woman, and there is no need to reply to the question. Father turns as red as his hair, pays with a large note. Mother looks down and discretely begins to weep. You are holding hands in a public place, sir, the waiter finally says as if the prompt reaction and payment by Father now required an explanation. But his words are not an accurate description, because the supposed misdemeanour is more about an arm admired than about a hand touched. And the waiter gives Father the change and Father leaves him a tip, smaller than he would normally give, understandably, but a tip nevertheless. Everything seems to be a matter of honour for Father and always will be, tipping included. Meanwhile the waiter is growing impatient. It is his job to make sure people vacate their table quickly, especially now that there is a long queue of Sunday sightseers waiting in the heat. And all this while, the sun is shining brightly over a city ever so darkly torn apart. In any case, it is the norm to queue: from queueing for a table at a cafeteria, where you can barely pay with a tenth of your monthly salary, to queueing for your daily subsistence and allocated rations. And Mother and Father get up and begin to walk away without looking back, for they have been shamed in front of all those sitting at other tables. *Humillados* is perhaps an accurate word, but more so is *deshonrados*. Head bowed down, that's Mother; and he, Father, lowering his eyes and thinking this was definitely not a good start to the budding romance. He would have liked to go back and explain: but waiter, holding hands and touching arms will not be such a big thing in a few years; in fact, it will be of no consequence whatsoever! He always knew that he was ahead of his time in everything he did. And in the case of Mother, she would have added that nothing is permanent, especially when it comes to practices, tastes, social conventions; and that it is best not to get stuck in the rut of traditions which will, sooner or later, change beyond recognition and be replaced by gentler and more equitable customs; but she realises that the present and overpowering mindset about marriage is so much more powerful than any intellectual notions she may have about how to live a good life; at the end of the day, people's opinions about you are fundamentally important, as she has been taught to believe. And that was the end of the story, because Father and Mother never again discussed what took place there that warm day, sitting outside a Madrid cafeteria, with an overzealous waiter. And if I happen know about this story, it is because Father told it to me at the end of his life, as if trying to cast aside the things that most weighed on him.

Because I did not explain, they did not know. I did not complain, so they thought I was content. I did not talk, but only listened.

I wanted to save my children from suffering, but it proved impossible because everywhere around us there was much going on to make people suffer. Yet having had to struggle this hard has made them into the phenomenal women they are today.

Elocution and deportment: first, I had to recite the classics (Lope de Vega, Quevedo, Garcilaso, and so on) in a loud and commanding voice; and then I was made to walk up and down the corridor at home, balancing several of those classic books on my head. Such are the signs of a graceful woman, Mother would explain without giving me a reason as to why I should become that sort of thing.

There I am at the seaside, surrounded by other youngsters. We are all fooling around at the beach. The adults are a long way off, and we feel they cannot control us, at least for a while. One of the girls sitting beside me suddenly shouts in excitement. She has found a ring among the many stones and pebbles that border the sand. We encircle her, wanting to get a good look at her find. It appears to be a pretty gold ring with a shiny red stone. Her mother has heard the shouting from a few meters away where the adults are and comes over to confirm that the ring is the real thing. She says that it is a proper ring and takes it from her daughter and lifts it to the sun. *"¡Con una esmeralda!"* she adds, *"¡Valdrá una fortuna!"* And then my mother comes over to where I am sitting and whispers to me things like why did you not see the ring before your friend spotted it, it was lying there just beside you and you missed it, you could have seen it and now we would have a priceless ring, you should be more alert next time so that you do not miss out on any valuable things around you, what are all these people going to think, they will say you are not clever or attentive enough. *"¿Qué va a pensar la gente?"*

Mother was always perfectly turned out, with exquisite dresses and high heels; not even her chipped tooth could spoil her aura of brilliance.

Toys: as well as my German toys, I had lots of dolls; I most remember Pierina, my first ever doll and which was almost bigger than I was, made of a very tough material, some kind of early polystyrene; and Gertrude, made of wood and with a purple dress and bonnet that made her look at least nineteenth century; and a huge doll, with womanly shapes and a dress in an Edwardian fashion, whose name I cannot recall; and of course my adorable little boy doll, already mentioned, and which I still have from birth, always sitting here beside me, as old as I am yet never aging, my very own Dorian Gray.

A strict Mother and a lenient Father is not a formula for success in the field of child rearing.

I attended a sci-fi film festival, and was in put in charge of PR, welcoming and accompanying famous individuals from the international world of film. In one of the evening events, the celebrated film director R suggested that I go up to his room. I replied that I was married. He said that he did not mind.

By then, the metastasis must have reached the tips of Mother's toes and the very top of her 70's hairstyle.

Grandfather rightfully used to say: *"No me dan miedo los muertos sino los vivos."*

There was a period in my recent life when my brain was on high alert and I was working intensely and without pause on far too many projects: editing and publishing books; tutoring amateur writers; writing and translating short stories; working on the Spanish version of a famous English novel; producing the webpages of a major Arts project; managing several accounts on social media as well as a couple of websites; formulating and formatting events, chairing them; being a judge in literary prizes; discussing potential conferences and organising some of them accordingly; being part of executive committees of various associations, organising their events and running their social media; preparing for interviews with slapdash interviewers; even putting up with heated conversations and having to listen to cold and unkind and unjustifiable words. Yes, I was working 18 hours a day out of 24, and sometimes longer hours if you can believe that. As a result, my blood pressure shot up and my mental stress became intolerable. I suppose this is what you would call burning the candle at both ends, and probably in the middle as well. Combined with the uncertainties of the pandemic, I was not in a happy state. The day after I finished the last of all these projects over many months, I suffered a series of strokes and was taken to hospital in an ambulance. It was sort of expected. They diagnose it as 'burnout'. I would call it a total breakdown of the world as I knew it.

"*¡A comer y a callar!*" they said to the children when their pet goose was served on Christmas Day. And the children wept desperately, refusing to eat and repeating only one word: "*¡Gansito!*"

Every morning, upon waking up, she created a perfectly curated image of herself.

Bereavement? What bereavement? I never went through bereavement. No counsellor, psychotherapist, physician, consultant, specialist, doula, ever asked me how I felt. I have only ever known bereavement as a very mellow sounding word.

Every great writer is a great deceiver, or so Nabokov claimed. One can always, of course, leave out the word *great*.

Mother wanted me to check a lump above her breast. And I checked very gently, and sure enough there was something there, unwanted and alien. She went to the doctor and within a few weeks a biopsy proved the worst. Soon afterwards, Mother's breast was removed, but the operation was carried out without counselling and certainly without informed consent. That is how things were done in those days –issues got sorted out quickly, details cut short. Patients had to cope with any amputations thrown their way without the necessary psychological support. And after they removed her breast, she made Father send a case of the best wine to the surgeon. Was it something to celebrate, I wondered at my young age? When discharged, Mother went on about the success of the operation and did not seem too bothered about the future. She even confessed to an aunt, who told me years later (in retrospect, I do not think I should have been told this particular story) that when Father made love to Mother after the mastectomy, he would say that he did not mind having just one breast to himself. *"¡Al menos uno!"* he would cry out, holding on to it as if raising a flag in victory. For an unsentimental army major, this must have been pretty passionate.

This is what I did when my children were away from home: I would lie on the beds of my absent offspring and smell their sheets and silently weep.

"Eres demasiado señorita, y lo mejor que te puede pasar es que te folle un camionero en la carretera de Madrid a La Coruña" –such were his words, delivered with a mighty laugh in front of several colleagues at work. This incident took place when I was a young broadcaster with a full-time job, whilst he was a freelance, had always been a freelance, would always be a freelance, would die a freelance.

Father used to tell us that the devil was out there waiting for us in some unrecognisable guise and ready to pounce on us at any unsuspecting time. The devil will appear in many guises, Father would insist, to tempt you and cause your downfall. What I am trying to say, he added, is that the devil is part of daily life, always there. But if you cannot admit the existence of a god without a devil, I suggested, this means the former is not self-sufficient and requires the existence of wickedness to prove that he or she can defeat it. I would come up with this sort of stuff rebutting everything Father said, but he always replied that I said such things because I was lacking in something fundamental: faith. *"¡Te falta la fe!"* he would exclaim. And I would retort: *"¡Yo solo creo en mí misma!"*

You could well say that the journey was much longer than anticipated and, as I had brought no books to read, I resorted to remembering the past.

I have muddled feelings, that is all there is to it. This sort of thing probably has to do with suffering tragedy without properly processing it. Let me explain: when something goes wrong I have an absurd belief that this is nothing but normal. Such a warped idea is the result of not wanting to part from what you know, like the warmth instilled by the shit that you have experienced in your life.

I would do both: perform remunerated work and also attend lessons whether at school or at university. I would go to school, and in the evenings I taught English privately. And when at university, with great difficulty it has to be said, I would also work for a radio station; then for a women's magazine (in those days it was more feminine than feminist, but it still kept up with women's developments politically, medically and socially); and then as a stringer reporting on student demonstrations; and then as assistant to one of the British correspondents in Madrid. I always did more than I was required to do. For some, as they said to me on many occasions, doing so much was just making things difficult for myself. But for me, it was the only way to live.

A WOMAN ALONE

No, she has not yet dealt with her grief. Is there a problem?

That mid-summer's day I played with my friends until late, so late in fact that I was afraid to return home because I knew Father and Mother would be upset. It was already ten o'clock at night, and I hid in our neighbour's garden. There was a full moon, and I remained sitting on a bench under a large mulberry tree. There is something about mulberries I love, and I like to think that they have looked after me over the years, whether with their shade or their delicious fruit or by keeping buzzing beasts at bay. And in that charming garden, under the full moon, I could hear the neighbours talking inside the house. It felt like I was no longer a little girl, but someone who could analyse what was going on around me and come up with an opinion of sorts. Was I perhaps turning into a mulberry tree myself? I could sense the rustle of the wind around me as if I were a real tree, with my arms as branches and my eyes as fruit; and all this time the full moon shining brightly over what I had become. From where I was, I could hear life going on as usual, with parents and children chatting, the clatter of dishes, the smells of a delicious supper escaping from the open windows. And I, a mere child of five and three quarters, was caught in the middle of all that, not knowing whether to go or to stay. By now, I thought, my parents would be so worried; and the more I thought about it, the less I wanted to go home. I stayed and overstayed. But I was beginning to get just a little afraid of the dark. I was sure that the mulberry tree also thought I should return home. This is no place for a little girl or, if you prefer, a young mulberry tree, and it caressed me with its leaves. I finally went home, only to incur the wrath of my parents. I thought they would be so very happy to see me. Instead, I was angrily reprimanded and received a slap that made one of my loose baby teeth come off its root. I was so distraught and felt so helpless, I definitely could not understand adults at all. It had definitely not been a wise decision on my part to return home. Next time I would not come back at all, I decided in my young and rebellious mind.

Translation into and out of, articles of association, radio scripts, journalism, features and critiques, conference documents, compliance terms, bylaws, fiction and non-fiction, expressions of thought, memorable quotes, birth announcements and obituaries, statements of fact, speeches both personal and political, patents, competition rules, legal guidelines, statutes of association, tool instructions, glossaries and lexicons, language learning material, directives, love letters, official proclamations, rhyming poems and non-rhyming poems, cogent exposition of ideas versus stream of consciousness, ethical standards and moral exclusions, guidance and advice on worthwhile or non-worthwhile subjects, suggestions and opinions and controversies, hearsay and rumours, hints and intimations, clarifications and obfuscations, definitions and ambiguities, texts and subtexts, language and metalanguage, standard discourse and slang, direct and indirect speech, synonyms and antonyms, coarse language and lyrical language, hyperbole and understatement, contradictions and agreements, metaphor and fact, conjecture and truth, hope and doom, sense and nonsense, the extravagant and the plain, enigmas, postscripts, the fierce and the tranquil, dilemmas and solutions, the frugal, the ancient, the naïve, the peaceful... She will write anything you like, whatever it may be, and much more so if you pay her.

During the ceremony, she so very beautifully read out Eliot's verses, and everyone understood that what he and I had was precious: "And the fire and the rose are one."

As I aged, there were things on my list of preferences that went from being the most thrilling to being the most undesired. Can you guess which ones?

Being on the losing side: one of my first and most cherished memories is the acrid smell of train stations. And this is because Grandfather was a railway station master. Or rather, he became a station master, for this had never been his childhood dream. He had always wanted to be a scientist and had in fact a science degree. As an adult he owned workshops and factories where he built those large old-style radios with a vacuum tube as well as musical instruments, among several other enterprises. And then one day, like in a modern tale, he lost it all because of new technical developments invading all industries. After that, he had no option but to get a full-time job with anyone who would offer him the opportunity, even if it meant leaving Valladolid and heading for Barcelona. I suppose working for the national railway company was as good as any other position: steady employment, with housing provided and, mainly, the possibility of considerable overtime. As promises go, some proved to be empty as we shall see.

My amygdalae are telling me to run away and never come back, and the frontal lobe is insisting that I stay and face the music. There is serious backstory to every side of who I am.

My reflexes are among the abilities I have lost to some degree as a result of strokes. I still have a reflex response, of course, but it is not the same as before. I am slower and more awkward in my movements. I do not feel robust enough, at least not just yet. I do not trust myself to be able to react in no time at all, as used to be the case. And as a result, I have stopped doing one of my favourite activities, and that is driving. How I used to drive everywhere, I would find it so elating. I knew the streets of London so very well, the parking places, the no-entries, the short-cuts. All gone now, and I am resorting to walking everywhere. I suppose I am now walking for all the walking I did not do before because of all the driving.

If you know me only in Spanish, you are missing the British half. If you know me solely in English, then the Spanish half is lost on you. But even if you know me in both languages, the elusive me is always a problem.

There are feelings that only exist in one language and not in another, and so it follows that you will never experience what those who speak a different language can experience. To take but one example, the word *cariño*, which can be translated as the feeling you have towards someone you possibly like, or you possibly love, or you are possibly fond of. But none of these three options is accurate enough to express the experience of warmth, wellbeing and contentment we might have towards someone when we feel *cariño*. It is not exactly about loving someone nor about taking a liking to someone. It is not fancying someone nor is it about developing an everlasting relationship. At the same time, it is not less than *love*, and not necessarily more than *like*. With fondness, you can be fond of tennis; with liking, you can like vanilla yoghourt; with attachment, you can be attached to your stuffed zebra; with love, you can call people 'love' when serving them a first course at lunchtime. But *cariño* is the overwhelming and otherworldly emotion that I feel towards my closest and dearest; sadly, some of them are incapable of understanding the word, let alone the feeling.

Yes, I admit I was a convent girl, raised by nuns, with religion –a most intransigent version of religion– as the basis for everything in life. No wonder I had issues.

My first serious piece of writing was a poem dedicated to Mother on her death. I was barely an adolescent, and what I wrote was tediously long and agonisingly sad. Love lost, nostalgia, remembrance, darkness, tragedy were my subjects back then, and I suppose they still are, though nowadays not always and not in this order and not necessarily as obvious as all that. The verses I wrote were much like a death poem, *jisei*, as someone would compose shortly before committing suicide, only in this case it was not my death but Mother's. Shortly afterwards, I remember burning my earliest poems, including that first one dedicated to her. Literally burning. I made a pile, and on the terrace of the family flat I stroke a match and saw all those sad words turning into ash. The members of my family were away that afternoon, and no one watching from the street thought it worthwhile to phone the fire brigade after smoke was seen bellowing from a first-floor balcony. The burning felt like some kind of redeeming and cathartic act, a way of breaking with the past and starting afresh. Or perhaps I was simply playing with fire.

I suppose some of you might want to know whether I shed a few tears in the process of writing this memoir, especially during the more dramatic events. I have to confess that, with all the heavy editing the book required (something like chipping off endless bits from a huge block of speech, which is your very first draft, and adding many other smaller sections to make the text clearer, all of it resulting in several hundred drafts), I was more or less anaesthetised to any feelings or emotions. In any case, I did all my weeping when these narrated events actually took place.

When we were out with Grandfather, he would always have a camera dangling from his neck and he would incessantly take pictures of us. *"¡Mirad a la derecha, mirad a la izquierda, en marcha, quietos, abrid los ojos, cerrad la boca, adelante!"* Sometimes Grandfather made me really mad with all his demands and his constant camera-clicking, yet now I am so happy to look at those endless snaps taken by him. *"¡Sonreid, niños! ¡Sonreid de verdad!"*

Earliest memories: a headless chicken running along the corridor at home and leaving a bloody trail behind it; a pig howling as it was being knifed in someone's back garden during the slaughtering season; a pet hamster hopping several times into the air before collapsing and dying after someone stepped on it while I was playing with it in my room; and worst of all, my pet goose being sacrificed for Christmas dinner. No wonder I did not like eating meat.

Everyone wants a stake in this war. The estranged husband says he is after a larger share in the joint life policies. The children want a bigger house. The boss, a longer report. The plumber, a shorter working week. Me, a more daring love life.

My colleague at work had a nervous tick which made him wipe his nose in sequences of four. He took four swipes at his nose, stopped for a while, and then started all over again. I suppose this is why his nose was so large, after years of being rubbed wildly on a regular basis. It stood out on his face like an oversized growth that did not match the rest of his features. When I was first introduced to him, he was rubbing his nose in desperation, and with me being so young I thought he was insinuating something inappropriate. Later on, I saw him doing the same thing in the studio when we went on the air and were jointly presenting a programme, and for a few seconds I assumed that he was trying to seduce our listeners across the waves. He had the most engaging radio-voice, with a calm manner and a self-possessed temperament to match. I have met a lot of individuals with radiophonic voices, but no one ever surpassed him. Our listeners were enamoured of the way he spoke; luckily, they never got to know about his nervous ticks or, what was much more serious, his warped comments about the dangers of migration in the UK. Yes, he was unfortunately a xenophobe. He even made such comments when we were on the air, especially when a news item we were discussing on our programme happened to be about migration: sometimes he spoke in a loud voice while a pre-recorded tape was running; other times, he mouthed his comments silently while I was reading the news live. *"¡Pero si tú y yo no somos nada más que emigrantes!"* I shouted at him whilst strongly pressing the cough-button.

She is not exactly a flaneur like Pessoa but does like to observe everything around her. With curiosity and respect, but rather sneakily. You would not even suspect that she has been watching you all this time.

Along the route I chose to follow, I got distracted far too many times. But it did not mean that I lost my way.

When Father remarried, we did not go back to normal family life as we had so much hoped for. In any case, we had not experienced normality for such a long time, after the years of upheaval with Mother's illness and death, that I suppose we had forgotten what it was like. Tempers flared when both the children and the new stepmother thought innocent comments were said because of them. It took me a long time to realise that a blissful home cannot be created overnight, and even more time to understand that being a stepparent is an atrociously demanding role. On the one hand, the children expect the stepparent to be a perfect substitute for their real parent, or even better; on the other, stepparents feel they are constantly failing because their very best never seems to be enough in the eyes of the children. We must accept that, in certain situations, there is simply no way out.

On my birthday, I was presented with a white-gold ring enclosing the tiniest diamonds so that I would not part from the bearer of the gift.

There is something called fatigue and, until you have experienced it, you cannot even begin to imagine the toll it takes on your body. It usually crops up unexpectedly after an illness or a medical condition, and it is particularly abysmal after strokes. No one ever warns you that you might be affected by fatigue. When it does make an appearance, you feel that your body has been hijacked by some indescribable force. It almost gives you a taste of death, for basically you cannot move, think or speak when fatigue strikes. You are left hoping that your fatigue will eventually subside and disappear but –and this is fundamentally important– without taking you away with it.

Part of my culture: loss and longing were not so much embedded in me as embroidered into me, making such a deceptively pretty pattern.

There is a wonderful word, *convivencia,* which refers to the ability to live with others under the same roof, even if it demands disowning yourself for the sake of harmony. I tried it so many times that I have become an expert at disowning myself and my desires.

I remember, I suppose, what I can remember, yet going forwards or backwards as I please.

Oh, how they made Spanish omelette in the post-war days. It was a Vegan's delight, without a single egg. Even without potatoes, as they were so very scarce. They took the pith of the orange and tossed it in oil, and then added water and flour and salt. And there it was, a Spanish omelette. A real pretend Spanish omelette for those hungry enough but who lacked the necessary ingredients. After the war, rationing was the rule, and the authorities handed out small sachets of unidentified powder to make dough and soups and creamy white sauces. I still have a few of those sachets. They were passed on to me, and I value them as part of my inheritance like an item of family jewellery or a photograph of ancestors.

Mother would say to us *"¡Sois lentos como vuestro padre!"* and complain accordingly: Oh, such unhurried reflexes, such sluggish intellect, such slowness of movements, such weakness of character. Unlike her, of course, because she was as fast as the wind, constantly processing information, aware of everything around her at all times, never once ceasing to think and mull. Yes, she was privileged enough to know so many things, she claimed; and because of such proficiency, contradicting her was totally out of the question.

Santa Teresa, among the first feminists: "*Así que, hermanas, todo lo que pudiereis sin ofensa de Dios, procurad ser afables y entender de manera con todas las personas que os trataren, que amen vuestra conversación y deseen vuestra manera de vivir y tratar, y no se atemoricen y amedrenten de la virtud."*

My dog was called Lucky. In fact, he was my brother's dog, and Saba the cat was mine. Lucky was, indeed, a very lucky dog. He had Saba as best friend, and assisted her whenever she gave birth, which was usually once a year. Grandfather would, at this time, take her new-born kittens and put them in a sack and head towards the river, but that is another and very distressing story. Lucky was loving and kind, and sometimes a little cocky. He had black fur and a golden patch on his neck; Saba had black fur and a white patch on her neck. His eyes were light brown; hers were yellow. Unhappily, they were separated at the end of their lives. Both were taken to an animal sanctuary against the wishes of the children in the household, who shed many tears. She, with abandoned cats; and he, with abandoned dogs. There are things that I will never forgive, and this is one of them.

I do not think that he wanted *me* in particular, with my many flaws and my smallish number of triumphs. What he wanted was a woman, with all that clichéd stuff that being a woman stereotypically entails: a sexual body, a motherly attitude, a patient and kind disposition. When he got to know me, he realised that I did not have all the predictable traits but offered instead a few others that he had not anticipated and which, in due course, made him question a life lived ever so conventionally.

On the subject of writing, from my story *'Tradescantes'*: *Asumir la ficción como realidad es común y necesario, pero no es desde luego más extraordinario que interpretar la realidad como fábula; los que así proceden (esto es, los que están convencidos de que las páginas de los libros llegarán a hacerse realidad un día no muy lejano) vivirán siempre un sueño a la espera de que se realice. Entretanto, los pocos que consideran que la realidad es ficticia o falsa o simulada (y opinan, además, que de publicarse como obra alcanzaría escasa difusión) sostienen que hay otras realidades que tienen más peso (nadie define tales realidades; en situaciones propicias se las menciona de pasada para constatar si hay alguien entre los presentes que piense lo mismo y, consiguientemente, proceder a un intercambio de información o, si se prefiere, establecer vínculos de mayor intensidad), y por ello no viven esperando que se realice lo soñado, sino que aspiran a que la realidad llegue alguna vez a tener la fuerza de sus sueños. Así pues, que los tradescantes existieran es innegable, pero no podría saberse con toda certeza si fueron como aquí se dice o como narran los historiadores (su existencia está documentada por eruditos de renombre, se tienen numerosos documentos que atestiguan la dedicación y diligencia con que se consagraron a su empresa; pese a ello su presencia en el universo es tan irreal que parecería soñada..., tal vez un sueño común, provocado por alguien que necesitaba de su existencia, alguien a quien le era absolutamente imprescindible creer en ellos)...*

In seeking comfort, you tell yourself that what you are living through are just stories along the lines of the fairy tales you enjoy reading. At age zero, you are born with a lucky charm on your head in the shape of a strawberry that might just provide you with untold strength; at age two, you run along the garden dressed in a red cape with a hood, confident that such an attire will render you invisible and impervious to pain, especially if there are any wild animals around like wolves; at age three, you find a black cat in a palace and decide to keep it, for it will surely turn you into an enchantress with supernatural powers; at age four, you find a strange tin recipient in your garden that might contain a genie waiting to be awakened by your touch; aged five, you have turned into a mulberry tree and no one will ever realise that it is you; at age six, you cross fields and meadows on your own because you are following someone who is playing a pipe and who will lead you to a secret magical place; at almost seven, you are given a beautiful white goose as a pet and you blindly believe that it will lay an endless supply of golden eggs, and when some months later it is is served for Christmas dinner you stop putting your trust so blindly in fairy tales.

This is a possibility like any other: she writes and, as a sideline, she lives.

Her lengthy and remunerated involvement in a global agency was killing her soul, as simple as that. Immersed as she was in the world of the real and the tangible, she felt oppressed and ignored because she longed for the world of illusion and fantasy, the only true one in her eyes. And when she realised that her life was becoming an irrelevant narrative with no room for elation of any sort, it became obvious that it was time to leave the place, and soon.

Father and Mother did not tell us too many stories about their suffering during the war, and I suppose it was to make sure that we had a happy childhood without experiencing sadness or dejection. They constantly kept us in a bubble of enjoyment and bliss for our own sake. And when things started going wrong in our lives, we took it badly for we had not known that distressing events could happen. If we had been led to believe that the world was for real and that fantasy was only for made-up stories, we would have survived a little better. But I should not complain: stories were the scaffold holding me together, giving me courage, allowing me to dream, keeping defeatism at bay.

And suddenly our Xmas decorations and nativity scene in the sitting room were set on fire by Father's shoddy electrical workmanship, and we had to celebrate in a room with offensively besmirched and buckled walls, much like where the original event took place.

After any event with lots of people, I am always asked whether I had a good time, and I never know what to reply.

In that particular photograph he was old, but you could still admire his gaze and his hawklike nose and his receding black hairline. You could tell from his lopsided smile that it was not sarcasm that lit him up but anger at the cards that life had dealt him, such an unlucky deal in his view; with his looks and intelligence he should have been prominent, famous, adored. And she was totally infatuated by him, and she meant that in the carnal sense and not as a niece was supposed to love. She meant it in the most lurid sense, in the most disorderly way. When he was alive, she loved him as only an adolescent can love. With all her soul, so swollen would her guts become with the sudden rush of desire. She should have seduced him just like that, and she thought of it many times. She definitely had opportunities. He would sometimes bring her home in the car after an evening spent with him and his family. Once he stopped the car by the river. You could barely see the water; it was that late. He looked into her eyes but said nothing, perhaps he was expecting her to utter a few decisive words. She was seventeen and could not bring herself to say anything other than: *"¡Cómo brilla el río esta noche!"* Nothing ever happened, and the potentially scandalous story was conveniently spun into an innocuous memory.

I am obviously paraphrasing: all extroverts are easily alike, but introverts have each their own particular way of being misunderstood.

My first disappointment was of a literary kind. It was a story told, and made up, by Father. He was the one in charge of telling us night-time tales and introducing us to imaginary worlds. The particular story I am referring to was about a magical moneybox (*un monedero mágico*) that had an endless supply of money, all of which produced great delight in us children. And after many weeks of telling us the same story at bedtime, one night Father said to us that the money inside the imaginary box had run out. But Father, I protested, you said the money would never finish, and he replied: Well, it did, because all things come to an end. Oh, my disappointment! It was almost impossible to get over it, and for several days I did not want to listen to another story by Father, and certainly nothing about the mysterious moneybox. As it happened, there were two serious mistakes in what I considered at the time to be a terrible fault on the part of Father. This was the first mistake: you cannot promise a child one thing and then not deliver, and I am referring to a box containing unlimited money that one day somehow fails to produce a single coin. And this was the second mistake, so much more serious and harmful: the love of cash, instilled from such a very early age.

Workwise, I was lucky in that I worked in multicultural and multilingual corporations that were not into making a profit. Their aim, at least on paper, was to improve the lot of humankind in one way or another. Accordingly, I was never a subservient employee exploited by shareholders or investors but was instead working for the world itself. There are, of course, other ways of exploiting and abusing staff, even if such organisations are not making any financial profits at anyone's expense. Sadly, the workplace, however lofty its ideals, is where certain people fully exercise their iniquities and, in some cases, vices, especially when in commanding positions. Almost without exception, all the bosses I ever had were total despots. But then I have encountered quite a few bullies in my private life as well, though for now let us not go there.

I am a recovering perfectionist: I am not on any type of medication, but I do need to lower my standards at least once a day.

When did I stop believing in Father Christmas, I hear you asking. In my case, it was the Three Magi, *los Reyes Magos*, and not Father Christmas. Discovering the truth about the myth was not too difficult. When waking up early on the morning of the Epiphany, we the children saw a note from the Magi explaining that the presents had been hidden in various places at home. And when reading the note, I recognised the writing as Mother's. Yes, her very distinct writing: slanting, elegant, neat, spidery. Either it was an incredible coincidence that one of the Magi wrote just like Mother, or the whole thing was one big lie. I said nothing, of course, and went along with the fallacy for the sake of both my younger siblings and my parents; the older members of the family seemed so much more excited by the whole thing than the younger ones. From then on, I always questioned everything parents said and did, but to keep everyone happy I would pretend that did I not realise what was going on.

Mother went to the doctor with a lump in her breast and was asked whether she was happy. But are you happy? Happy, the doctor repeated. Happy as in happy? Yes, happy as in content, elated, thrilled. The word was *feliz*. And the question was: *"¿Es usted feliz?"* Even in those days doctors suspected that your frame of mind might well have to do with any sickness you developed. And she replied that she was not necessarily overjoyed, but certainly expectant. But as to happiness, she said that she would not know because she did not really think she was entitled to such wonderful things. She assumed that, in a way, she could be considered happy, with her little amusements and inconsequential observations, living in her own small and manageable world. However, happiness was far too big a word, and an even bigger state of the human spirit, she added, and perhaps she did deserve to be happy, given that she had given so much to the world... She went on and on, as she always would, saying far too many things, most of them unwarranted, but not really providing an adequate answer and, worst of all, not wanting to deal with the truthful answer to that important question as posed by someone who was trying to get to the bottom of things.

Oh, what would I give to live with reckless abandon. Instead, I have to make do with constant doubts, revisiting my decisions a thousand times, conflicts cramming my core until it shatters, with pointless questions about the future and with achingly unnerving memories of the past.

Aged four, I visit my elderly aunt's huge country house in a village near Valladolid, where possibly a mild case of coprophobia was born. It was the result of having a serious tummy upset after bathing in an open tub and catching cold; and then the results of the mishap: uncontrollably defecating in the middle of the night in the large dorm, surrounded by all these older cousins whom I barely knew and who were woken up by the mess. Everyone in the house was up, old and young alike, the lights were switched on, the women in the family became suffocatingly over-demonstrative, the children made faces at me, Mother quickly changed the sheets but did not look one bit pleased, the stench was agonising.

And the more I settled for the expected, the more unsettled I became and the more I ached for the unexpected.

Even the protagonist of her own story has no idea about how the plot is going to unravel.

And as mentioned, Mother's third child, a little girl, my Sister, was born in a London hospital. The following day, Mother asked the Charge Nurse to please pierce the baby's ears because that is how they do it routinely in Spain with new-born girls, thank you very much. And the nurse opened her eyes as far as they would go and said: "For the same price we can also pierce the baby's nose, if you wish." That sort of reply would today be considered blatantly xenophobic and culturally insensitive. But Mother's request could also be viewed as highly prejudiced; a child should not have anything done to her body without her consent and only once she reaches an age when she can think and decide for herself. My Sister had her ears pierced many years later and, because she almost never wore earrings, the piercings eventually faded and disappeared into a faint memory of both intolerance and prejudice.

He was made from a diverse assortment of elements. I think this is probably why her feelings towards him were contradictory. You could easily see that he was compassionate, but then detached; attentive, but not emotional; broadminded, but not carefree; physical, but never sensual.

I asked the specialist to check my episiotomy, and he complemented me on the texture of my skin, which is not exactly what I was asking. "You really have very good skin, and you get that from your mother," he said, to which I replied nothing. My body was in a position that not even sex partners have ever seen me in. Legs up in the air, buttocks protruding, my pudenda open like a fresh flower under the morning sun. The doctor examined me thoroughly and slowly, and then gave me his views. Spectacled, safe in the comfort of the colossal leather armchair as used by authorities on medical subjects, the specialist looked not at me but at the world beyond me, the world of science and progress. He asked how he could help me, as shop assistants ask in department stores. And I valiantly answered: "I can only do it in the missionary position." He heard my reply without batting an eyelid. There was no apparent reaction on his part and so I thought I would explain, perhaps he had not heard of the missionary position, as odd as this may sound for a man who claims to know so much about the insides of women. "The straightforward way is the only way for me, so I really can't," I added looking at my left, "have any sexual contact from behind or the side," and I looked at my right, "and I find it all too painful, I just can't," I said looking at my knotted hands on my laps; and I added finally, postulating as the conclusion what I had provided as the headline, "I can only do it in the missionary position." It was then that he reacted. He opened and shut his eyes several times, and he finally directed his focus towards me. I was now in the line of his sight, but speaking to me was far less interesting than speaking to the whole world at large as he had done when I entered the consulting room. His lips opened, and still he said nothing. He produced an inscrutable grin as he finally proclaimed: *"*And is that so important?" Yes, he said those words: "Is that so important?" I again looked at my hands on my lap, at my feet side by side on the floor, at the window from where one could have a brief glimpse of the vast expanse of Ravenscourt Park. "No, I suppose it is not," I said, when I should have taken him by the lapels of his white coat and made his chair swivel, "no, it is not all that important. At the end of the day, it is possibly unimportant. Totally unimportant. What is important, anyway? What?" We had come to the end of the consultation. And when opening the door to leave, I looked at him for one last time and realised that I had not said anything about his impudent comment. My reply should have been: "It is for me to decide whether a sexual position is important or not, whether missionary, preacher, or proselytiser, whether I want to have sex in a certain position or no position or half a position or not at all!" No, I did not say what had to be said, and it took me a long time to turn thoughts into words that cannot be silenced.

After having admired the picture in my study for so very long, I realised that Utamaro's 'Laundry by the River' had been completed just before his death.

Mother wrote her little poems and articles in the company magazine under the pseudonym *Mis B* (*Mis B* and not *Miss B*, as such were her initials). She had won various typing and short-hand and drafting competitions at national level and was highly regarded as an administrator and very much respected and trusted as a colleague. Those were of course the 1950s, an unrecognisable world to us today. And when Mother went to see her boss to announce that she was shortly getting married after having been engaged to Father for several years, he said that he would give her a dowry, just like her *papá*. No chance of keeping my job, she asked, and her boss looked at her cautiously and got up from his chair, with his hand gesture inviting her to leave his office.

For sure, I can do neither small talk nor Big Art anymore.

Despite the heavy influence of religion throughout my younger years, in due course I learnt to reject any type of faith in unproven events. I do not believe in anything beyond life itself or, even better, in anything beyond the absence of life, because life was not always part of the universe as we know it. It has been an inorganic universe for most of the time, and it should return to that state of affairs one day soon.

My friend N keeps repeating the affirmation that explains it all, the sentence that passes sentence, the theme, the motto, the prayer: *"¡Todo se reduce a un sueño!"*

What a stupid thing this high-grade sensitivity is: everything hurts so much more, unnecessarily so; and what is worse is that life becomes unliveable at times.

If someone were to ask me how it was that I fell in love, I would say it was his touch: when holding my hand, his warmth shot through my skin at prodigious speed and ended up nesting in the depths of my body and, decidedly, my mind.

Some more paraphrasing: Whilst I am telling you my stories, I am managing to stay alive just like that other storyteller.

The school report clearly said that I was belligerent. I did not know what the word meant until I started learning Latin at the age of ten, when I realised that 'belligerent' came from the word *bellum*. In fact, when learning the full declension for 'war' we would sing a little wordplay: *blum, blum, blum, bli, blo, blo, bla, bla, bla, blorum, blis, blis*. But neither knowing the meaning nor singing the tune made me feel any happier. Being called belligerent was like a sentence passed, as if there was no redemption in my case. I felt I could do nothing to erase belligerence from my life, stuck as I was to that word. Would I have to honour it and be belligerent or argumentative or even loud-mouthed for the rest of my existence? All this went through my mind for a very long time. Anguish, as felt and displayed by the young, is no small thing.

That piece of hardened lava I always have beside me when I write I picked up from the summit of Vesuvius.

Entertaining all these conflicting feelings towards other people stems from having had parents who are unfair with you and, five minutes later, are back to being loving; they get terribly angry and then they kiss you as if to seek forgiveness; they punish you harshly and the next day they buy you gifts; they raise their voice, and then they sing you a lullaby.

Do not feel sorry for me; it appears that I sort of worked it out in the end.

Grandmother always kept the most beautiful geraniums in a large balcony on the first floor of her house. I never saw a dry leaf on them, nor any dry blossom, nor signs of sickness, nor invasions by parasites; and certainly never any rust spots or fungal disease or dark pustules or bacterial infections. Nothing was how it should be in her life, yet her geraniums never once let her down.

Cascarrabias: what a wonderful word! Grandfather was definitely a *cascarrabias*, he said so himself. The word 'curmudgeon' might be a good translation but not quite, because the Spanish term can be applied to you at any age, and the English word is reserved for much older folk. I think that, at this stage in my life and having gone through quite a few unpleasantries, I am gradually turning into both.

I was raised by nuns who taught me to love both Language and Art. My sole contribution was to add an adverb: *unconditionally*.

As to the subject of writing, it is a kind of surrender: ideas enter your mind uncalled for, though not necessarily unwanted because you might find them exciting, or at least mildly pleasing; and then you give in to them, allowing them to take over who you are and how you live, until you eventually put them on a page in the right order and with the right frame of mind. Now, for example, I have surrendered to a new idea: a scheme between a prospector looking for gold and someone who knows that there is not a single gold nugget to be found in the surrounding territory. They speak openly to each other; the first one talks about the possibilities of exploration, the second about the certainty that they will find nothing in their search. Despite all, they decide to join forces and embark on an adventure, crossing that vast land by foot, on a horse-drawn cart carrying with them their tools and several hand-drawn maps that they purchased in a nearby town. Essentially, the purpose of the ill-starred journey is to prove the other one wrong. And then I realise that all this could be the beginning of a moderately good story called 'Prospectors' or 'In search of gold' or possibly 'What is it that you are looking for and that is nowhere to be found?'

Until I put the past to rest, it was always ready to grasp me by the throat.

Seeing all things in terms of drama, or even better, melodrama: is this the seed for an author, or simply one tough and miserable way of living a life?

So here I am telling reading to my children. Spot the mistake! A simple storybook telling the story of Snow White, awkwardly illustrated and with a narration plagued with errors and inconsistencies. On the one hand, I taught the children what to look out for and to find the mistakes in the story and the illustrations, laughing all the way; this was probably not the best thing to teach young souls. Oh, but on the other hand, lying down with a child on either side holding tight to me, whilst reading together stories and constantly laughing was the best thing ever, ever, ever... Nothing, really nothing, compares to it.

"What is a nice girl like you doing in a tyrannical system like this?"

Living to tell the tale: I suffered two acute small infarcts in the region of the superior cerebellar artery (left paramedian cerebellum and left superior peduncle/left inferior colliculus of the tectal plate), plus subocclusive stenosis of the left dominant vertebral artery and occlusion with soft thrombus in the left superior cerebellar artery. All of this was followed by a brief transient ischaemic attack or TIA some three months later, which made me realise that I had suffered several of these TIAs in the previous couple of years before the actual strokes as warning signs but had paid no attention. So now you finally know what happened to me and why I was not up to communicating with anyone or saying anything, or why I was thinking that I had nothing to live for anymore.

One day I left the house and walked for ten miles straight without knowing where I was going. I ended up in A&E, cursed with anxiety, riddled with guilt, stricken with uncertainty.

As a child I was taken away from a fascist dictatorship to 60s London, and I could not believe such freedom was possible. Then as an adolescent, I was taken away from London and returned to a fascist dictatorship, and I thought that I had been condemned to some kind of Underworld. A few years later, after university, I got a full-time job in London and returned, but only after having witnessed what fascist dictatorships can do to people and countries, and more so to your young mind and your blossoming dreams. Freedom is what we must live for, and if you have to move away, whether from countries, people, ideas, situations, time spans, then so be it.

Let me tell this in case you have not realised yet: it is not that artists create a *persona* for their art, but quite the opposite; artists create a *persona* to live in the real world, trying so hard to fit in.

Here and now: nothing more than a smallish planet spinning off a star and ending up with all the right ingredients to sustain, by some fluke, life itself.

I say this without regret: I may be too old; it might be too late.

Sporadically I have these out-of-body experiences when I am about to sleep. I float around my room and then return to my bed within a minute or two. But every so often, I float beyond the room and into the street, and then above the trees and the rows of houses. Yes, I have been known to fly towards the sky. On one occasion, I even hovered over the coastline of a frozen and unrecognisable land. I sensed the freezing air in my nostrils and the droplets of moisture on my skin. And after flying around for a while, I got tired and went back home. Once in my bed, I wiped the frost away from my eyes and covered myself with a blanket from head to toe because I was feeling so very cold. Is this an amazing astral trip or a simple reverie? Let me know what you think.

All those loved ones who died, did so during particularly hot summers. For some bizarre reason, scorching heat and death seem to go together. Thus, I so much enjoy cool English summers, rainy August days, fresh seas, bouncy clouds.

Whenever I tripped or hit myself accidentally, Mother would say: *"Dios te ha castigado."* I could never understand the reason why I was being punished by these supreme deities, for I was always trying to be a good girl. *"¿Por qué?"* I would ask. And she replied almost without thinking, placing the onus so terribly on me: *"Ah, tú sabrás."*

The orphanage in central Madrid, the so-called *Cotolengo*, where middle-class schoolgirls were taken to visit deprived children for an hour in what was part of the curriculum. In a group of about twenty girls, we were led to a huge and icy hall where dozens of little kids were running around us and screaming *"¡Mamá, mamá, mamá!"* The children so much hoped that we would be their mummy and would take them away forever from that dismal place. They all had an identical bowl cut, a cream coloured overall and the same limited vocabulary. And we, young and pretty and ever so spotless, were at a loss as to what to do. We wanted so much to embrace all the tiny helpless children but had been told not to for fear of contagion or getting soiled. And in that soulless hall, the woman looking after them, huge in size and temperament, would forcefully wipe their snot on her apron, for the little ones were cold and some of them were most probably sick. *"Mamá, mamá, mamá..."*

There is a picture of me in hospital, standing beside the bed, with my arms placed on my huge abdomen, just moments before giving birth. I look as I if I am about to die, but I can assure you I was smiling to the camera.

And publicly I read a little script of mine about two lovers saying goodbye. My dear friend C, a magnificent poet and actor, played the other role. The performance took place in a rather solemn setting in front of a large audience, and yet I was draped with only a bedsheet. Why did the two lovers in the story break up? Simply because the woman had found someone else. And this is why she says: *"¡El amor ha muerto, viva el amor!"*

To believe that you, a mere simian, can engage with none other than the creator of the whole universe is nothing if not utterly farcical.

The usual suspects: they are such melancholy memories that you cannot seem to shake them off even with four sessions of meditation a day.

Upon me they unremittingly inflicted a fear of Hell. I think they went that far because eternal life was not enough to make the idea of being a good girl genuinely attractive in my eyes. I enquired about the subject of Hell and Heaven a good many times, and I was told in no uncertain terms that wrongdoings would condemn me to eternal fire and good deeds would take me unambiguously to cushy clouds. All simple, tidy, seamlessly structured. Yet I was not really convinced that my sanctity −were I to achieve it one day in some mysterious way− would get me a pass to heaven, or that my childishly wicked thoughts would condemn me to the Netherworld. It was easy to come to this conclusion when you observed bad people misbehaving and getting away with it, and good people leading a life of virtue but dying like everyone else.

Am I the descendant of those who stayed behind but carried on with their beliefs in secret? Over five hundred years later I still feel persecuted, as if mine were a remote and clandestine identity and, within my mind, I had to furtively bury the annals of my ancestors. That kind of history is very much present in every one of my surnames, which at the time had to be changed to more common or even Christian-sounding ones in order to avoid persecution. From those surnames it would appear that I am but a direct descendant, from both from Father's side and Mother's side. But how can I prove it decisively? Well, look at me and my wandering.

A boyfriend of mine used to say that he and I were not of this world. Is there another world, I would keep asking him.

Final exams. On that day particular day, Mother Superior decided to dramatise the very tense moment even further. What she said was utterly gratuitous, but it probably made all the other girls feel better, luckier, privileged. Just before we were to take the exam, Mother Superior stood in the middle of the classroom and spoke out loud, walking towards my desk and rudely pointing at me with her right index finger as if I were a total outcast: *"¡Ayer enterró a su madre!"* Yes, it was exactly the day after Mother had been buried. And there I was, about to take my final exams, all eyes on me. Me, a girl still coming to grips with Spanish, and the range of emotions it allowed, and the hyperbolic usage of the language, and the indefensible but culturally necessary comments in times of tension. A few of my schoolmates looked confused, but most produced a sigh of relief from knowing that they were not in my place. I was at a loss about what to say and thus remained silent, bemused in fact. I took refuge in my mind, where else. Mother Superior had used an unfortunate exaggeration, painting me as a sinister undertaker doing the digging and burying of Mother. And this was the scene I imagined: a dark mountain slope at exactly midnight; a storm splitting the skies with lightning and thunder; me firmly holding a spade with both hands and digging a large hole in the ground; and alongside me, Mother's dead body in a shroud, waiting patiently to be buried. Back in the classroom, I became so very anxious that I could not help but burst out laughing, in fact rather loudly. The looks from all the other girls, and especially from

Mother Superior, were now of utter loathing. In most cases, black humour has a very distinct beginning.

I was once told off because my decolletage showed unimportantly. The person who told me off was a woman; a feminist, as she immediately described herself. I am both a woman and a feminist as well, I replied.

Mother would endlessly repeat: *"Que no te conozcan."* The realm of the private, the sanctity of your secluded self, the unshareable core of your existence. May no one ever get to know you!

"Si te publico esta novela te hundo," a publisher once said to me. Who knows what would have happened if she had published my novel, a copy of which I no longer have, neither can I even recall the plot or the characters or a single scene. No, I cannot find the manuscript among the endless electronic files, hundreds if not thousands of passages, stories, dialogues, acts, that I have written over decades. In any case, selling books is such an unpredictable business and if they had published my novel, perhaps I would not have sunk but floated all the way to the top. It would have certainly saved everyone involved a lot of time and, mostly, pain.

I have such early memories of mulberries, aged three or four: Mother would ask what I had been up to looking at the stains on my hands, and there was no denying. After that, there was no denying anything when Mother asked, with or without the stains.

As was customary, they performed a *soixante-neuf*, and then he said that he wanted to make her come the regular way.

He would achieve it, he boasted, one day soon. What is the *regular* way, she asked.

I would have this dream as a child, repeated almost daily: a terrible and wicked sorceress would arrive every night to ask me if I wanted to be her child. If I said no, she would take me away. And if I said yes, she knew I was lying because she could read my mind, in which case she would also take me away. This was the first dilemma of a long series of dilemmas throughout my life: whatever I did, I was doomed.

As a side-line, she lives.

Father's nickname for me was *veleta*. He would say that I unfailingly changed my mind all the time, just like a weathervane on top of a roof; and I replied that it was because I quickly grew out of things when they started to bore me. I admit that sometimes my tastes changed so much from one moment to the next that it felt as if I had turned into a different person, almost without acknowledging what came before. Father would explain that my character was thus because I was a spoilt little girl. If anything, spoilt by you, I retorted. And trying to put an end to such recriminations, I claimed that it was probably all due to a sudden evolutionary change. *"¡Como si la mente no pudiera experimentar mutaciones, papá!"*

No one ever asked her the right questions, so she seems to have given the wrong answers.

And so, this is what aging is. I had always wondered what getting to old age would feel like, and I found out so much sooner than expected. Losing interest in the superfluous; becoming in no small measure pretty acerbic; experiencing the progress of scepticism running along your spine; reconciling with the fact that you will lose everything in the end without having achieved what you most desired, at least not completely. And yes, finally beginning to live life to the full.

Rejections? Tell me about rejections! Most of what I have written has been rejected, not once or twice, but several times over. Even this book was rejected on a number of occasions. Initially rejections used to weaken and upset me. But in time I learnt to react differently, freeing my soul to welcome both rejections and acceptances as incidents without any real value or usefulness or purpose in the wider context of writing or in the even wider context of living.

There can be songs without words: John Field's Nocturne No. 13 in D minor.

Though her life was intricate enough, she always pursued plainness: coming alive under the sun, the simplicity of a flower, the dexterity of a bird.

The bad news: my story did not get selected for a short story competition and was therefore not included in the book they published with the stories by winners and runners-up. The good news: I turned the story into a long sci-fi novel, the first of a series, with a heroine who could single-handedly beat all the odds despite the many setbacks in her life. The worse news: the book did not sell as expected. The better news: the heroine in the book inspired the author to get on with it.

The land you choose to be buried in, she said, is your true nationality. And I replied that, according to her theory, I could not really tell what my nationality was because I did not want to be buried in any particular piece of land. Buried at sea is a good option, I said, especially in an area over 200 nautical miles from the nearest coast. This would be the high seas, which belong to no one unless a particular country wants to stake a claim for what lies underneath such waters. That is where I want to be buried, the high seas, because I too belong to no one.

What a rotten waste of life: how many generations had to die in order for you to complain so much.

I had forgotten about the following episode and was reminded by someone who witnessed the encounter: a minute after the ceremony, my left foot was stepped upon by his right foot. This was an old custom on his part, a sign that a man would always impose his will on a woman and that the woman would say nothing nor complain, as young and unknowing as I was at the time.

The first draft of my first ever novel was produced by literally retiring from the world for several weeks, convinced as I was that I would be ecstatic once it was written. During that time, the house was not cleaned, food was not bought or cooked, children were not fed, phone calls and emails were unreturned, post was unopened. And when I finally had my first draft, I can tell you that ecstatic I was not. And even after twenty years of working on that book, ecstasy did not once enter the equation.

These days I would say that I am more pugnacious than belligerent.

In public you must be unflappable, and nothing must perturb you, Mother would constantly say. Once, when crossing

France by train, we were queuing for breakfast in the restaurant car. I was making funny faces and even funnier voices to get my siblings to laugh. Mother detested my pranks, considering them unfitting for a girl, and so she slapped me in the face in front of the many passengers there, even though I was already twelve and menstruating. Following her advice to be unflappable, I kept my cool and did not shed a single tear.

He wanted me desperately but decided against the idea of us being together –he was far too pragmatic and decided to stay put and leave things unchanged in his life. Oh, but how I wanted him. One word from him, and I would have left everyone and everything. After all these many years, I am so very glad that he did not say that word.

After the funeral, I was not crying as much as people expected –in fact, I was barely crying at all. I remember coming home and reading her will, a spiritual will if you like, for there were hardly any material gains resulting from Mother's death. It was hidden in her handbag and it read more like a farewell letter than a legal document, as if she suspected that she might die but did not really expect it to happen to her ("*¡A mí, esas cosas no me pasan!*" I could hear her saying, as I delivered her words); even on her death bed she was playing to the gallery and never admitted the possibility of a final defeat. And as I was reading, I remember having to keep my feelings in check as the eldest child that I was, for my siblings were too young and Father had never really known what to do in emotional situations, as undemonstrative as he was. In a matter of minutes, I had to grow up so very quickly, as if forcing myself to cross through a tiny opening into the unknown world of adulthood. At the same time, I could not help wondering why a youngster like me had to deal with all that gloomy mess when I should be having loads of fun, going to clubs, falling vacuously in love, absconding school, smoking anything thrown my way.

Has she lived backwards, now having to deal with the consequences of decisions she took when she was not yet ready to take such decisions? It turns out that the life she now leads was chosen by a younger and inexperienced version of herself. She can do little but follow genetic paths, pushed around by the hormonal mayhems to which a young mind is submitted to, pay dearly for choices taken so resolutely early in her life without sufficient evidence.

What happened was that she, a senior member of the family, decided that the portraits of Grandfather and Grandmother were far too large for her sitting room and had them trimmed. Thus, the striking background of the outskirts of Valladolid were lost from both portraits; this, from a sentimental viewpoint. From a material viewpoint, the signature of the well-known portrait artist of the time was also gone forever. In any case, you could never cut down Grandfather and Grandmother to size, as they had always been larger than life in my eyes. I now have those portraits, hanging along a section of the staircase at home – just their superb faces, with no context and no background and no artist's signature. Whenever I go up or down the stairs, I ask both portraits for sustenance and inspiration, and I always have the feeling that they are not giving me the full and unedited answer.

Cervantes wrote a novel called *'La española inglesa'*, published in 1613, in which the protagonist, Isabela, thinks instead of saying things out loud.

My first name is not necessarily my own but the result of custom: all daughters, especially the first born, were to have the same name. This was an unwritten rule in the family. Perhaps all my female ancestors and I do not just share our name but other traits, character included. And it could well be that my thoughts and wishes, just like my name, were also borrowed from previous generations. Nothing but the tiniest link in a such a very long chain going back in time am I.

Yes, I have experienced some dark nights of the soul; and no, you do not ever get over such nights.

For years and years, Mother's father worked overtime for the Spanish railways without any of it ever being paid. In those post-war days, the country lacked funds to keep the whole reconstruction process going; clearly the fascist propaganda machine was expensive to run. Thus, overtime owed to state workers accumulated to heights unknown. Yes, the subject of Grandfather's outstanding overtime became the family running story, even a tragically entertaining one: when Grandfather is paid all the overtime he is owed, we will be able to afford this or that for the whole family, holidays, a bigger house, a new car. *"¡Las horas extraordinarias!"* Grandfather eventually died believing that the huge amount he was owed would, at the very least, be paid to his heirs. That first generation of heirs has passed away. And now it is down to us, the second generation, still waiting.

Grandfather and Grandmother were more anticlerical than atheists. Yet when Grandfather was about to die, Grandmother said to him: *"¡Guárdame un sitio al lado de las estrellas!"*

A view from the past: there is a woman housed in a small room with a window under the stairs in an old block of flats; she sits on a tiny stool, surrounded by packs of needles, reels of fine thread of many creamy hues, and a large magnifying glass. For a meagre amount, she will darn and mend your nylon stockings. The results of her work are outstanding, and no one will ever know that you had a ladder or a run on your tights. In time and with progress, however, what she does will cease to have any value and her profession will disappear, as will many other professions also performed by women. This is but a small homage to whole generations of working women to whom we owe a debt of gratitude, their contribution unjustly considered negligible, their replacement viewed as indispensable for the advancement of society, their sacrifice unrecognised.

This hopelessness is no more than my usual lack of expectation at all times of the year, virus or no virus.

The survival and success of the English language is the result of constant evolution, simplicity, adaptability, few rules, no gender. Should we then all move in that direction?

Even at an early age, I would scrutinise what I saw, paid close attention to people's expressions, tried to guess their emotions, remembered their stories in minute detail. What the purpose of all that was, I am not so sure.

Yes, darling, you are The One!

A WOMAN ALONE

—163—

IMPRESIONES.

Unas veces: ¿para qué?
Otras: ¡hay que trabajar!
Otras: ¡no podré llegar!
Algunas: ¡si llegaré!

—

Muchas veces: ¡me he cansado!
Otras muchas: ¡no se alcanza!
Muy pocas: ¡tengo esperanza!
Una tan solo: ¡he llegado!

—

Muy pocos siguen serenos,
desfallecen los demás,
tornan llorando los más,
llegan riendo los menos

—

Hé aquí la eterna historia
de los que juzgan posible
abrazar á la intangible
forma vaga de la gloria.

FLORENCIO BRABO

8 Octubre 1880

A poem by my great-uncle, Florencio Brabo

A WOMAN ALONE

The cut-out painting of Grandfather

The cut-out painting of Grandmother

A WOMAN ALONE

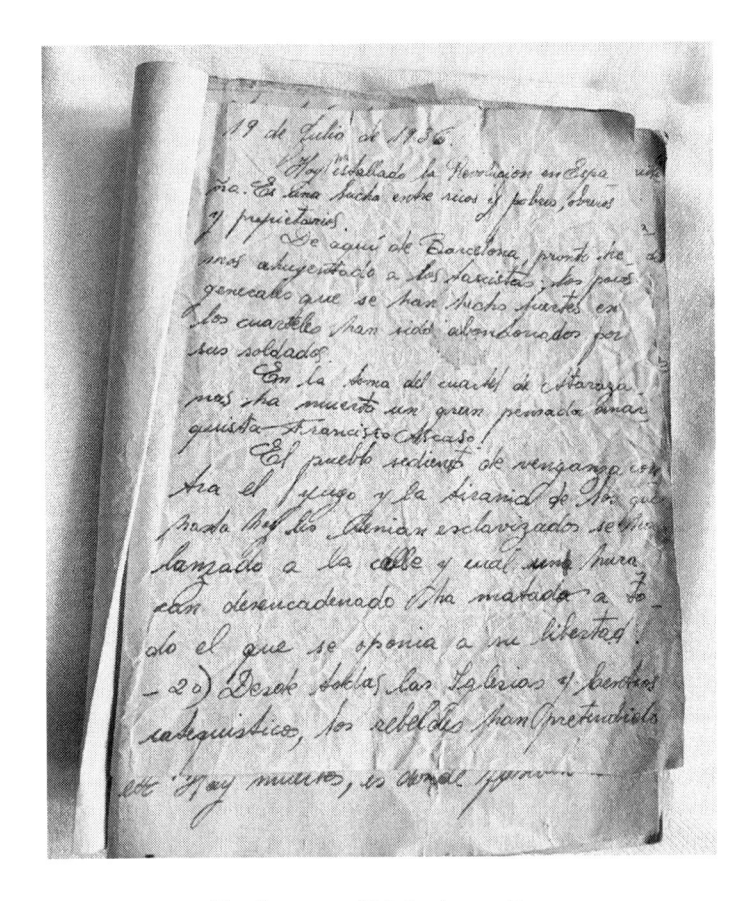

The first page of Mother's war diary

Isabel, my mother; Isabel, my grandmother; Sola, the family dog

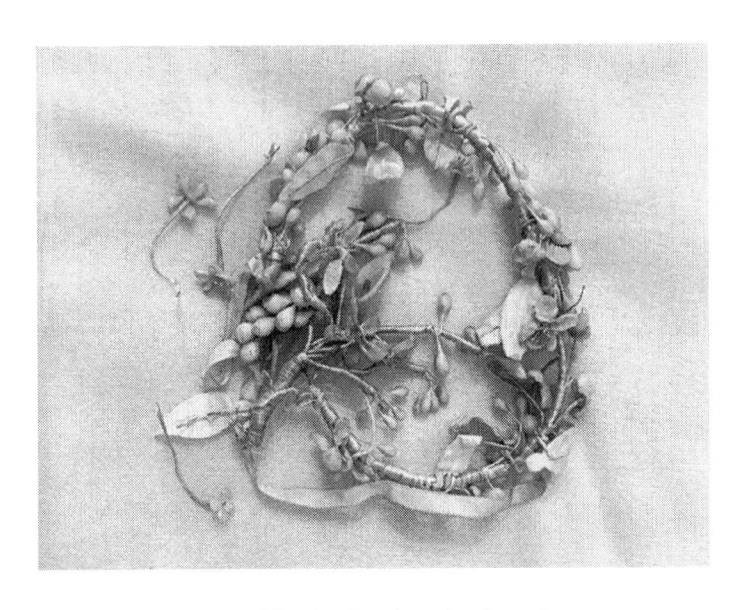

Mother's wedding headband, made of wax flowers

My strawberry and I

A WOMAN ALONE

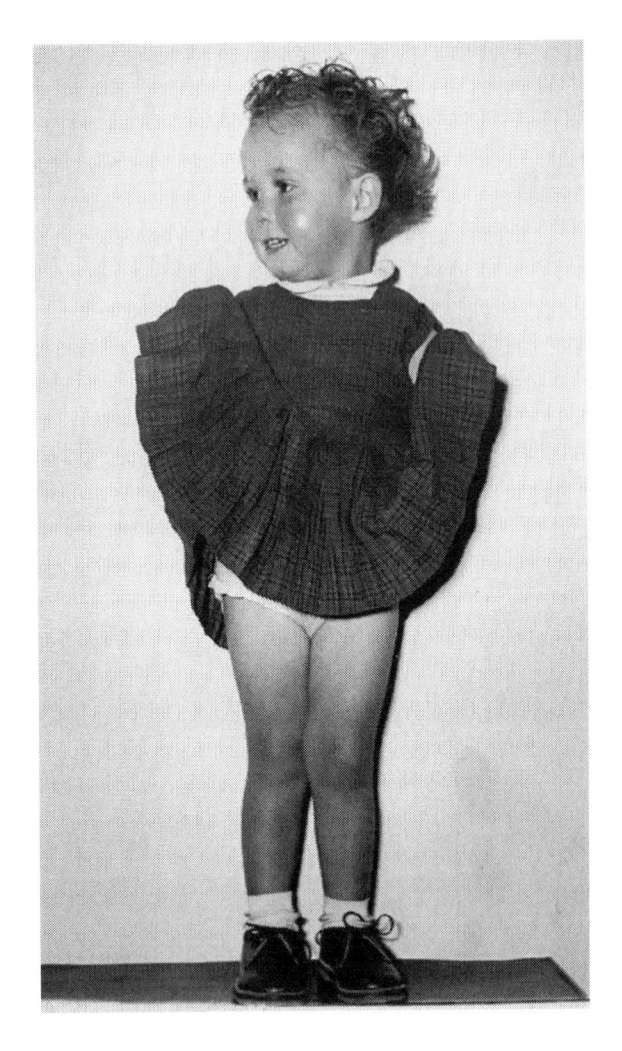

Aged two, learning to fly

Prep School in London, Isabel playing the triangle, with her own stand

Censorship: tearing off the last page of our magazine

The long way ahead, in Exmouth

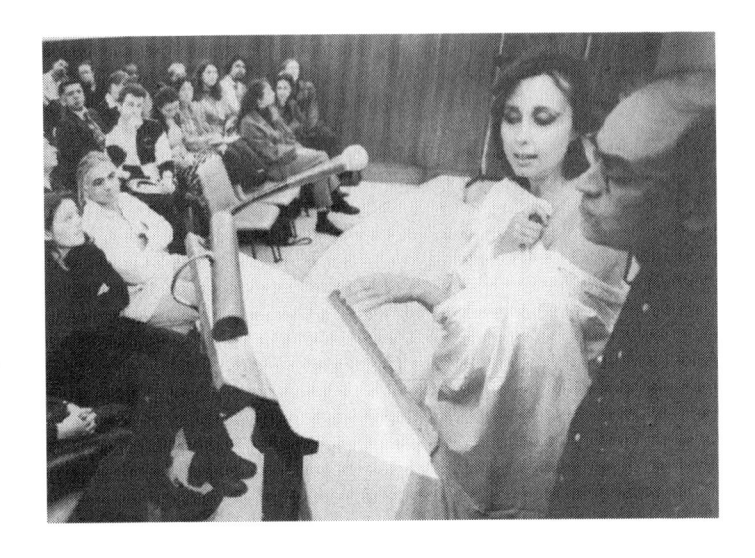

Reading poetry, at Canning House, London

Mixing with Royalty at Bush House

A WOMAN ALONE

Madrid, the city where I was born, with statues of the greatest ever writer and the two greatest ever fictional characters

In my study

A WOMAN ALONE

My paternal Grandmother's bracelet, the only thing I have from her

My favourite candy

A piece of tile that I found buried in the riverbank

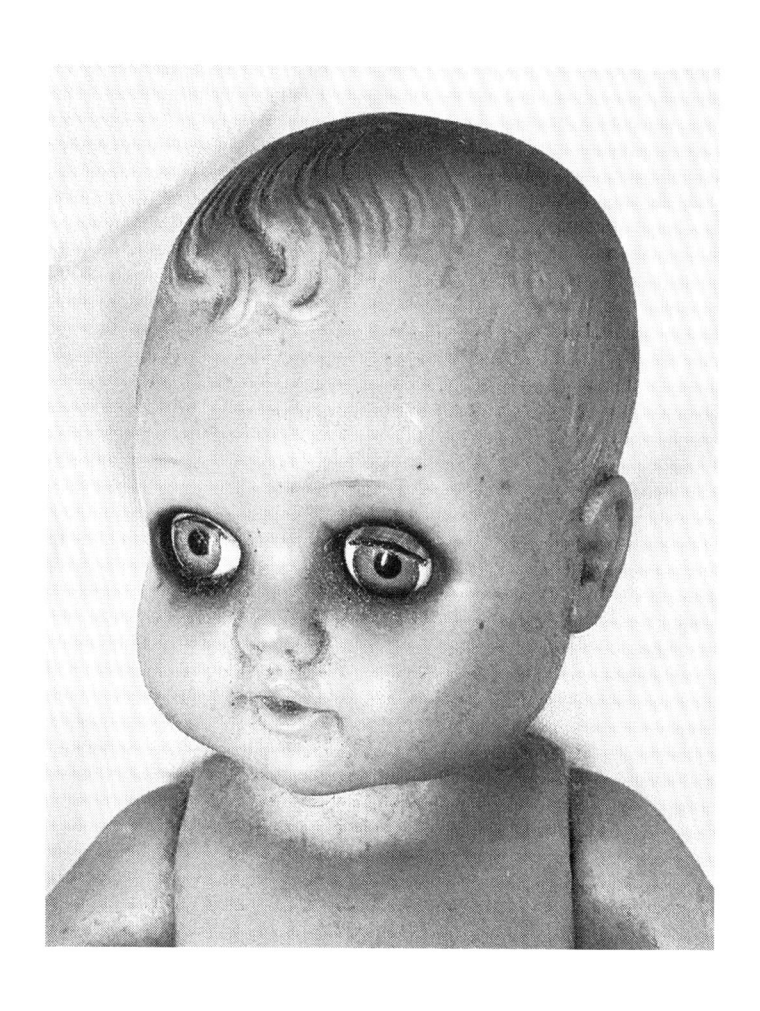

My favourite doll: as old as I am and still a baby

A WOMAN ALONE

Mother's stilettos

A WOMAN ALONE

Calling for help with my bell

A WOMAN ALONE

My three monkeys: do not speak, do not hear, do not see

My rosewood fisherman, trying to fish without a rod

A WOMAN ALONE

I like to have some of my favourite objects close to me when I write: a drawing of Mother, a jellyfish made of glass, a rubber duck, a piece of lava from Vesuvius, a small statuette of a laughing Quieci holding a bowl for good fortune, a tortoise doubling up as a pencil sharpener, and a large plastic clip in the shape of a sweet fish

A WOMAN ALONE

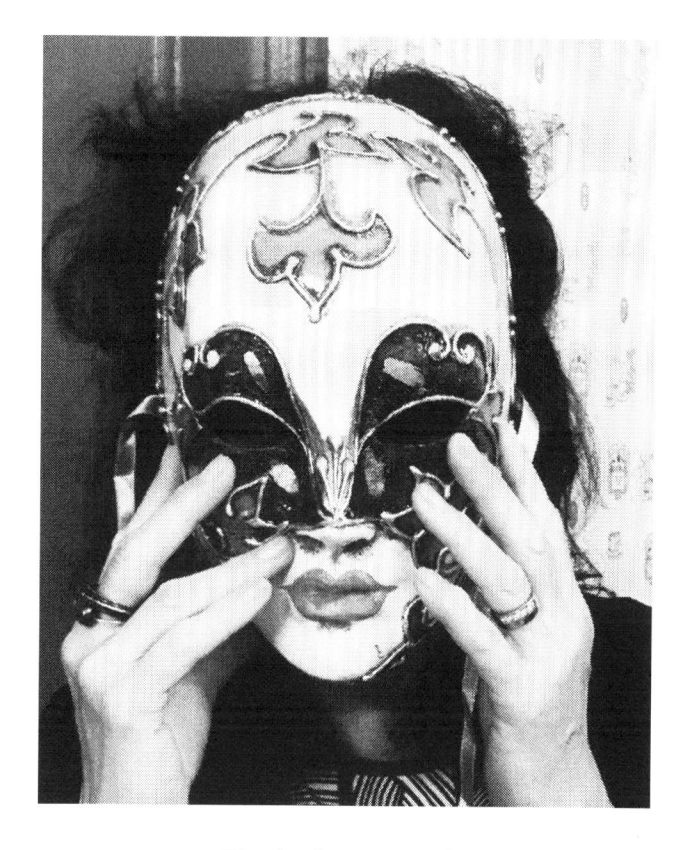

Wearing the wrong mask

A WOMAN ALONE

Unmasked

A WOMAN ALONE

This will not sell, the literary agent says. Literature in the UK is neither experimental nor intellectual, he adds.

I can do three things: complain bitterly about the rain, hope that it will soon stop, or put on my shiny new mac.

Any occasion is good to reassess your life: after watching a sunset; after declaring your love; after going for a long swim; after brushing your teeth; after lunch or after supper; after suffering a stroke.

I comb her hair, from the roots to the ends. Her tangled hair, pretty rings and satin curls are all laden to the brim with lice eggs like tiny diamonds shining under the glare of my nit-searching torch. Every louse-to-be dodges my fingers as I attempt to push them outwards towards the end of each lock of hair, riding and sliding on the clusters of dark and shiny strands, so clean from washing and combing, so gentle and soft to the touch because this is a small child after all. Lice prefer clean hair is what the chemist says as he hands me a new preparation, just out on the market. But then lice have become immune over the years to most products, he adds as he returns the lesser change of a ten-pound note. I take home the knowingly inadequate potion, pour it over my child's wet hair and wait. I have to wait for ten minutes, but then decide to give the bugs a couple of extra moments for total extermination. After nearly a quarter of an hour –the room immersed in an aroma resembling decomposing roses bathed in putrid vinegar– I am now ready to dispose of the bodies. As I was warned, the potion does not seem to have fully worked. But at least the lice are not hiding any longer now, moving around freely in the public square of my child's lovely head as if aroused from their slumber. But I will not be defeated. If I cannot do this chemically, I will do it manually. I take this finest toothed instrument and patiently comb each section of hair, hoping that the black remains of all those lice will show on its white teeth. With each stroke, out come the tiniest diamond-shaped eggs and the most savage of lice, many still alive and some temporarily collapsed under the powerful effluvia of the potion which in some cases seems to have half-worked. I even manage to capture a few of the large and flat egg-laying females. In just a few generations, they have become resistant to anything thrown their way, as evolution demands, except for the fine-toothed comb and the utter patience of Mother breathing heavily over her beloved child's hair for hours until rendered senseless from exhaustion and backache. Night after night there I am, hoping to achieve a nit-free atmosphere at the expense of my forbearance. When I think that I have achieved something close to success, I will possibly overlook but a single egg, which within a day or two will hatch producing an inkling of a louse, which within a few days will grow up to be a reputable reproducer, a mother of lice, and a mother of mothers as well, a blessed creature that can fulfil its biological destiny and intent on this business of laying eggs like pearls on the finest hairs of a sweet child who cannot understand why they chose her. Nor can she understand why they exist. Why do they exist, Mother? I cannot reply to my child's single, simple question with talk of survival of the fittest. I say: Shush, I can see an egg, stay perfectly still while I run my fingers smoothly down a strand of hair and feel the minute egg's curves and loops, its unevenness, it diamond-shape, its crevices and fissures. I am trying to develop Finger Intelligence, and on the cushions of the tip of my thumb and the tip of my forefinger I was never able to feel with such intensity before. But by now I have developed this fine art, this oversensitivity. Will this feeling permeate to other territories? One could say, for instance, I am as sensitive as someone who feels nits between the tips of her fingers. That is as sensitive as anyone can get, I would say. Sensitive and daring and warring. I am ready for bloodshed, I shout attacking a louse mother (or is it a mother louse?) with my bare hands, pick her up with two fingers, look at her twitch, and then say go and lay your eggs somewhere else. She is flushed away under the tap, and I look at the disposal of her wriggling body in excitement. Am I trembling? But I see no more mothers now, they must have run away at the rustling of fingers along the scalp, like a giant scoop in a jungle. And when I finish sliding one more egg down the strand of hair, my child shuffles for she knows it is time to move and shake before the next egg comes up for removal and she must remain perfectly still for a few more minutes. It is then that she remembers to ask again about the purpose of nits existing, the question I had earlier dodged. I do not have a reply for my offspring this time either, hunched as I am with eyes wide open on the look-out, a gigantic predator about to jump on its millimetric and oblivious prey. Then circumstances felicitously prevent me from exposing my inadequacy as a supplier of good and proper replies to questions made by inquisitive children. Out pops another egg when I shine the light of the torch on it from a different direction, and the question remains unanswered. It deserves a single comment, a silent one as well. You nit-picking bastard, I say to myself.

There are the bits of me that you can see in these pages, and then there are the unavailable ones.

Perhaps I should embrace all things around me as a spiritual retreat instead of going off to one.

The journey through this place of mine will take you to

countless doors, for there are always so many more doors to open, so many more, all leading to so many more rooms. And yet that is not intimacy.

The iconic photograph: him looking towards the East and her looking towards the West, but it was not only a geographical divide.

The catastrophism with which she was born, and which comes in so very handy for writing melodramatic scenes, is such a nuisance when she is supposedly trying to lead a normal life because even the tiniest misunderstanding means the end of the universe as she knows it.

When writing her stories, she used a distinctive perfume that was imperceptible to her readers.

To get someone to fully satisfy your needs depends on how well you voice your wishes. And what if you like taking refuge in silence, I hear you asking, and expect the other side to guess what you most enjoy?

Reinterpreting Camus, in the midst of chaos I understood that there was within me an invincible stillness.

Invited to a birthday party outside London, I am ten years old. My parents insist that the present to my friend should be one of the flamenco dolls they bought last time we were in Spain on holiday. It is a life-like doll, about twenty centimetres high, wearing a bright red dress with white polka dots, in a beautiful dance pose. I am driven to the party, and I give my friend the doll and she loves it. Halfway through the party, we go upstairs to her room to get some toys, and there, on the mantlepiece, is an identical Flamenco doll, twenty centimetres high, wearing a red dress with white polka dots, in a beautiful and identical dance pose as the doll I have just given my friend as a gift. It looks like a much older and dustier version, of course, but it is the same doll, yet another example of a mass-produced figurine aimed at tourists. Perhaps my friend had been to Spain on holiday, although judging from how old the doll seems it was probably bought a long time ago during a visit by her parents or even her grandparents. Obviously, the factories churning out these dolls have not changed the prototype for ages. I could not help feeling embarrassed and I said pointing at the older version: "Oh, but you have exactly the same doll!" And my friend replied most graciously: "Now the two dolls can be sisters!"

"¿Eres mujer?" The doctor asked me. I did not understand the question. Do you have periods would have been an easier thing to ask a thirteen-year-old.

Ah, Karma. When I was young, he imposed his family on me. When he was old, she imposed her family on him.

Dear earthly Father, why did you forsake me?

Una castellana seca y curtida...

At university, he and I had been so very close: travelling to places together, discussing books we had bought and poems we were writing; we ran side by side in student demonstrations and cleverly avoided being caught by the police, almost sheltering each other; we were considered the intellectuals amongst our classmates, even meeting clandestine political factions that wanted to recruit us;

instead, we invested our efforts in founding the first poetry group that had existed in the campus for decades. Our day trip to Toledo had been the most memorable moment of our close relationship. I remember that on the riverbank I found a piece of a broken tile not unlike those in the local museum. Nothing happened between us, as in sex, but we were undeniably as intimate as if in a romantic relationship. There was a particular word that had brought us together. I used it first, and then he had agreed with me that it was the only valid explanation of what was happening in the country at the time. The word was *nihilism*. I used that word, when eighteen, as he and I were chatting one morning after class, and he thought that it was the best word ever to describe the reality of living in a dictatorship. And the friendship was sealed over a single word. Emptiness. Nothingness. Barrenness.

Paulina and Seneca: she followed him to the end, but it was to be his end and not hers. Thus, she lived beyond what she was prepared to live. Each one of us must perform a different act of courage: for some, it is death; for others, it is clearly life.

Either La Pasionaria (I once saw her in the flesh, heard her speech, cheered her), Che Guevara or Emiliano Zapata said this: *"¡Más vale morir de pie que vivir de rodillas!"* It is not clear who said it first, but does it matter?

Tell the truth when writing but do not forget the aesthetics of it all.

Father's older sister had been a nanny for a wealthy aristocratic family that left for France during the civil war, and eventually returned to Spain. She had looked after the children of the family with her life and had essentially saved them in Paris by posing and pretending and lying, but that is another story. Because of such a feat on her part, the wealthy aristocratic family promised to compensate her somehow for her services during the war, and they spoke of giving her a valuable painting. A small canvas, an etching, probably discarded by the artist, nothing more than a study. Apparently, it was a work by none other than Goya. There must have been many discarded works by well-known artists over the centuries, entirely unclassified and not included in catalogues, perhaps even unsigned, works suspected to be fakes but as true as the masterpieces housed in museums. My Aunt would always say that the painting would be for us, her nephews and nieces, though we never knew with any certainty whether she had ever received it. At the end of her life, in a hospice, most of the things she had in her wardrobe inexplicably disappeared. To this day, nothing was ever returned or found. I am sure the painting would be one from Goya's dark period, one of his black paintings, a sketch, a rough outline, a rushed work, in thick and murky charcoal, telling us as he always would in his works about historical crimes that were not resolved in his day nor almost two centuries after his death.

What I want to do more than anything is to live by the seaside, I REPEAT, by the seaside. But that seems to be another story.

There is bay in Alaska called Disenchantment Bay. Which one of these two do you prefer: *Bahía del Desencanto* or *Bahía del Desengaño*.

How can it be that, not believing in ghosts nor in the afterlife, I hear a frantic knocking on my bedroom door in the middle of the night?

A WOMAN ALONE

The four elements: the winds of fate thrusting us around like defenceless Autumn leaves; the persistent rain of destiny that we cannot shake off from our skin; the flames of chance burning down our every desire; the earth of our ancestors wanting us back as soon as possible

My three monkeys: do not speak, do not hear, do not see. And for total peace of mind, I would add a fourth one: do not think. I am not sure, though, how this could be represented.

Until I got used to Spanish, when I was told *"¡Vaya rostro que tienes!"* I would look at myself in the mirror; and if they said *"¡Te has puesto las botas!"* I checked my feet; and with the sentence *"¡Te viene como anillo al dedo!"* I would spread my fingers and examine them closely.

Many millennia ago, introverts probably existed to prevent their tribe from taking too many unnecessary risks and from acting impulsively without considering all the various options. Nowadays, introverts are still doing the same sort of thing, but their cautious approach to everything is generally frowned upon. What is then our role today, and what our purpose? We await your replies.

It is a little sad that the only proven cure to any ailment is Time itself.

At that age I certainly never saw a shrink. And as expected, the sand was settled, shaped and moulded; solidified in one word. It was possibly too late for me.

A WOMAN ALONE

When at a very young age I discovered movies, I decided that Mother was Paulette Goddard and Father was Leslie Howard.

Typewriters: I still have Father's, a Hispano-Olivetti, Studio 46, circa 1940; but I no longer have Grandfather's, an older Hispano-Olivetti that was very sadly given away to a female member of the family. She did not want it for herself but to house it in a mini museum that had been created for her elderly boss in her place of work. He was a celebrated and wealthy notary in Madrid and had made up his own story with other people's belongings. I have always wondered how many other lies he used in the course of his very distinguished and highly acclaimed career.

If I love tapestries it is mostly because Mother made small ones, the size of a cushion. I have attempted to make them, and almost finished a couple of them, but eventually I grew out of the hobby. They require such hard work, one stitch at a time, and for a very long time indeed. So, I desperately wanted to see 'The Lady and the Unicorn' tapestries at the Cluny, one of the most remarkable works in both beauty and technique, and was fascinated by the inscription from the last of the series: "*À mon seul désir.*" The lady can be seen renouncing her jewels and placing them inside a small chest, with a unicorn on one side and a lion on the other. In the images depicted in the previous five tapestries in the series, she also seems to be forsaking her desire as manifested by her five senses. This is my interpretation, probably because it is a story reflecting much of who I have become. But you are welcome to your own interpretation of the legend: whether the culmination of a life, the disavowal of material things, or a love story beyond what can be seen, heard or touched.

The most passionate scene from 'High Noon' is in Spanish. Katy Jurado says: *"¡Un año sin verte!"* And Gary Cooper replies: *"Sí, lo sé."*

Father drove as if he galloped, shouting vociferously and unkindly at other drivers. No wonder his favourite insult was *'Babieca'*, the noble horse of El Cid. He screamed the insult through his open car window at anyone who dared disobey traffic regulations, or at least his own interpretation of traffic regulations.

The person I could have been is nowhere to be found, and yet I think about her so much all day.

When Father left his role as an officer, he became a dedicated children's writer. As an expert translator and specialist in children's literature, he had translated both 'Alice in Wonderland' and 'Alice through the Looking Glass' into Spanish. He was an incurable anglophile, but there were other reasons for his admiration for Carroll. He always claimed that the world was a wondrous and miraculous place, and that the pursuit of anything exciting, like a white rabbit perhaps, might take you to a new and captivating realm, and that even upheavals and ill-fated events, like falling through a rabbit-hole, could well be an awakening into the land of your dreams. Father had been an accomplished artist as a youngster, winning national competitions from his tiny town in Northern Spain. Sadly, when the image of a *déshabillée* woman appeared on the church wall, he was publicly blamed and shamed since he was the only known artist in the locality. Who else but him could have drawn that little masterpiece, with intimate minutiae, a desirable pose, a suggestive countenance? His father was none other than the Secretary of the Town Hall, and in a terrible rage he took away all of Father's drawing implements, crayons and oil paints, easels and canvases, and had everything destroyed in a show of public humiliation; it happened outside the family home, in the street. Father's career as an artist ended there and then. It was one of the most tragic episodes that Father would have to live through, and he would always say that the world of make-believe was the only true one for him, and certainly for anyone who was misunderstood or unacknowledged. When he told me this story from his youth, we wept together.

Is she different, special, unique, extraordinary, or just neurodivergent?

The party in power was called *Falange* or phalanx. I have omitted its complete name here so as not to give printed space to fascists, but you can always google it if you are interested. Its symbols: a series of arrows (representing the union of kingdoms) and the yoke (representing agriculture), images dating back to the Catholic Monarchs, Fernando and Isabel, in the 15th century. The party was in power from the end of the war until the demise of the dictator, but its influence on so many aspects of life has never been totally eradicated.

Delving into paradoxes: a poet longing for silence, a lover wishing to be alone.

My red lacquered shelves in the shape of a Moon Gate, but that is another story.

How was it for you, because personally I did not to feel a thing?

Student protests were rife at the time, and a few of my university friends ended up in jail, some of them for months. As the dictatorship was approaching the end, it became more lethal than it had ever been. The many appointees of the repressive Francoist regime were panic-stricken, and their persecution of dissenters turned even more ferocious. Despite international protests, there were a number of executions, two of them carried out with the medieval garrotte (though this capital punishment goes back to Roman times), where the neck of the prisoner is crushed. Multitudinous protests ensued throughout the country. One particular friend betrayed my group by giving her address-book to the police, and we suffered difficult months. The police needed names on which to place charges of any kind to prove that the government was fully shielded against what they considered to be destabilising elements. In class, a handful of fellow students were informers (we called them *"sociales"*). They were so boastful and arrogant about the services they rendered the authorities that they did not even deny who they were. One of them was manifestly clever, and to ingratiate himself with us he would talk about how the regime would soon fall; the other one was thoroughly stupid and loved to show us his gun; they both ended up with top marks and a high-level degree. No, you could not trust anyone; likewise, no one trusted you. Things were frantically political in a country that allowed only one party and one ideology, the theories of which we were taught at school as a compulsory subject, and which I talk about in this memoir. In those days, university was the only environment where political parties, though considered illegal, existed and were intent on recruiting students. The Maoists tried to recruit more than any other group, and they had a highly intelligent blonde leader who managed to do exactly that. Other groups struggled to attract numbers but then they showed much less enthusiasm: the Communists, the Trotskyists, and the Marxist-Leninists. I said to everyone that I was mostly interested in writing poetry, and they would snigger and reply *"¿De veras?"* My approach seemed to keep everyone at bay, but police informers were always one step ahead. They suspected all students, especially the poets, and would say that poetry hid political messages, which it probably did, more in those days than today.

I used to find it so comical when he said that tragedy was very much my thing.

My daily and stoic walk through Nature.

Until I did all this, it was impossible.

Translation? What is the subject? Who is it aimed at? What are the source and target languages? What is the context? What is the purpose of the message? Is there, in any case, a message? So many questions open up in your mind well before embarking on a new translation of a particular text. Yes, a bloody sport. You get your hands dirty and, as if that was not enough, you are unashamedly accused of being a traitor, a word that some like to say is a misspelling of 'translator' in certain languages. Ultimately, translation is about changing apples into pears without anyone noticing. To transmute, acclimatise, rewrite, re-erect. The worst is that you can never be entirely satisfied, who can with so very many options around you, uncertainty as your best friend. In terms of language, it is also a matter of taste, concern, time, complexity. It is entirely up to you to interpret whatever message there may be in the original text, if there is a message or an ultimate meaning or a second or third or umpteenth reading. A dirty, bloody, never-ending process it is. A lonely act, perhaps even a lewd one! Translating? Yes, take a piece of writing, kill it, skin it, pluck it, remove the bones from the flesh, slice it up, crunch it, destroy it to the core. And then what? Well, then it is the inverse process. Reconstruct it as best you can, try to rebuild something with all those fractured morsels, structure it and make it into a self-contained product if you are lucky and resourceful enough. And then, as a final act, give it the breath of life, nothing less. No, the target text will never be the same as the source text! No grass will ever grow back, that is a given, yet daisies will sprout. Daisies and chrysanthemums and peonies; a whole garden in fact, different from the original but a garden nevertheless. From one language to another, as smooth a transition as from air to fire. And if you are good enough, no one should ever know how it came to be. Worse still, no one will think a human was involved in the process. It happened by magic, without effort, just like that. Yes, so very easily.

You see, this is something that only the narrator and the reader know, but none of the other characters.

Mother's favourite word was *indudablemente*. Being such a long word, I suppose it allowed her to think for a little while before responding to the type of questions she hated.

What is it that is worrying her: this treacherous virus; the lack of a proper and urgent health response by governments; the increasing social injustice and discord; the bleakness and the anguish as felt by all; the thrashing of your dreams? Or is it all of the above?

Another example of a contradictory upbringing: warm, nurturing, loving parents, who bought us lots of books and took as to fascinating places and museums and historical sites and made us fully appreciate the beauty of Nature around us; I particularly remember with great fondness our outings to look for fossils in Maranchón. Yet, at the same time, they imposed harsh and arbitrary and absurd societal norms that would make your soul shrink.

Long-term relationships are tough on desire, particularly on female desire.

At age 11 my favourite TV programme was The Twilight Zone; my favourite artist, Rogier van der Weyden; my favourite writer, Guy de Maupassant; my favourite sweets, *bergamotes de Nancy*; my favourite colour, black on maroon; my favourite subjects, not the ones I learnt at school.

Menses started just like that. Initially, I thought I had a wound inside my groins, for no one had warned me that I would eventually get periods. After a couple of days, Mother appeared in my room, in her hand a foul pair of pants from the washing. The encounter was formal and to the point. Mother asked me if the pants were mine. Whose could they be, for I had a brother and a baby sister? Feeling guilty and ashamed, I replied: yes, those pants are mine. I admit it! And she said this, and only this: *"Se llama menstruación. Te vendrá cada mes. Sirve para tener niños. Te dolerá."* And she opened a cupboard in the bathroom and, taking out a very long gauze covered with a mesh, she cut a section from it and handed it to me. I would visit that cupboard once a month; Mother always kept a fair supply of gauze in the cupboard, so there was never any need to ask her for more. I mostly wanted to enquire about what menstruation had to do with babies, but I dared not. No, the subject of menstruation was never discussed again. Oh, I forget. There was one more conversation. Had she not said that it would hurt? Well, hurt it did, indescribably, on the first day of the cycle especially. That phrase Mother had used when so briefly explaining the whole process to me was like a sentence imposed: *"Te dolerá."* I did ask her once to give me something for the pain, and she replied that I had to put up with it; if you take any medication, she added, your future babies might be born with deformities. And that was the end of that. So, in winter I would press my abdomen against the radiator in my room to soothe the pain; warmth was the only thing allowed me. But when summer came, I had to endure the throbbing torture while screaming as silently as I possibly could. No one ever suggested the simple solution of a hot water-bottle, but perhaps that could also endanger the health of future generations. At the time, even the smartest women were wound up in old wives' tales.

Why not translate it as: *"Estar o no estar, ésa es la cuestión."*

Two futile actions: Father wrote a bilingual dictionary on military terminology that was never published; to make ends meet, Mother went back to work shortly before being struck down with cancer, typing addresses on envelopes.

I do not know what it is about the mouth of the dead. Of all the facial features, it is the mouth that definitely betrays death. When the mouth is concealed under the shroud, you cannot tell just from the eyes about the bearer's death; even if the lids are sunk, the person could still appear to be fast asleep or as having passed out momentarily. But the mouth is simply too crushing, clearly confirming like nothing else that the person is, simply put, a corpse. It could be because the set of false teeth cannot be fixed properly in death, or the tongue is too thick with *rigor mortis*, or perhaps the muscles holding the chin have collapsed nearing the end. Never look at the mouth of the dead for it is the ultimate proof of their demise. In fact, when you look at a dead mouth you lose all hope of ever regaining your loved one, and it is then that you experience total defeat in the face of death. Yes, the mouth is far too connected to life and all life stands for: where food is eaten, lips are moistened, words are uttered, laughter is heard, throats are cleared, liquids sucked, kisses deposited, sexual organs aroused. In Mother's case, the mouth also meant her piercing voice; her imperfect smile because of a chipped tooth; the clicking sound she used to make with her tongue to call both her dog and her children; the disdain in her lips for all things exasperating, which happened to be most things.

I now desperately need to quote the following by Quevedo: *"Burlas canto y grandes veras / miento, que yo siempre he sido / sermón estoico vestido de máscaras placenteras. / Del donaire en mi ficción / cuido, pues, quien fuere sabio, / que lo dulce sienta el labio / y lo acedo el corazón."*

You could say that I am going through a well-overdue episode of adolescent rebellion, which I was denied because as a youngster I had far too many responsibilities and duties. But that is an easy way out of the conundrum of my revolt.

Stop what you are doing, for this is the perfect moment: the warmth of your room, the sound of a fast train in the distance, the many pink clouds crossing the sky, the smell of bread that your beloved is baking in the kitchen, a reader scrutinising the fragments of your life and possibly dissecting them.

La ceniza es lo único que queda hasta que alguien se la sacude finalmente.

An uncle of Mother's died in an ETA attack at a cafeteria in *Calle del Correo* in Madrid in the 70s. He sold stationery to the police on commission. He had just held a meeting at their HQ about new supplies. After the meeting, he went to have a coffee at the ill-fated cafeteria, and that is when the bomb exploded. I had only met him once when I was a young child. He was a good man, as I understand. But it is always risky to do business with the enemy.

What was I to do when I found out that my child had been groomed, abused, raped? In those days, for it was very much in those days, all was kept quiet to avoid a scandal that might have ultimately harmed her. I was in a permanent state of shock, but more so because I was advised to say nothing. What was I to do but write a story about how, in seeking justice and finding none whatsoever, the female protagonist commits a violent murder to avenge her child.

I hear you asking about what I was doing when I heard of Kennedy's assassination. When they announced the terrible news, I was a young child watching TV. In a state of shock, I ran to Mother's bedroom –pregnant with my sister at the time, she was taking a nap. I shouted in English: "They have killed President Kennedy!" And she replied in Spanish: "*¿Y para eso me despiertas?*

Here I am, returning as an adolescent from freest London to oppressed Madrid: wearing Biba, a very tight ribbed white sweater, a shocking-pink kilt, white leather boots with a knotted flap, and a white quilted mac with a matching fedora. Yes, here I am, all dressed up like a sixties child but living in a fascist tyranny. People stopped to look at me in the street, perhaps in admiration but more likely in shock. Until I arrived in the city, I did not know that there were rules for what you wore, and particularly for what you thought or did. It was a tough time in the country for everyone, but more so for the young. Yet, by wearing harmless but dissenting clothes, seeds were sown and cracks appeared. Concede we did not.

During a visit to a Pow-Wow in Montana, the Apache participant strikingly attired in eagle feathers, and stirring as gracefully as a raptor, did not wish to be photographed by me lest the camera should carry away his pure and beautiful soul.

Who says it was not a fully-fledged love affair? I mean, I fell in love for ten whole minutes to be precise. Goodness, the intensity of it all crushed me to the point of suffocation, but luckily not for long. And all because he sang a song during the break of conference I was attending; I forget which conference and where and why, for my memory of that day is reduced solely to his singing. It was an enchanting and tender song from my youth, I had not heard it for decades. And the song did it: so beautifully sung and with such feeling, it softened me beyond all measure, mostly because I was not expecting him to know it by heart. And when he finished singing the song, it was all over; we both went back to our very regular and exceedingly tedious lives. It was exactly a ten-minute affair, as I mentioned earlier.

Mother would so wonderfully prepare the house in readiness for visitors: exquisite canapés and *medias noches* from the best local patisserie filled with the most expensive ham; very low lighting; incidental music, usually Chopin preludes, for she had quite a collection of easy-listening classical vinyls. At those times, the house turned into some kind of enchanted place for the most discerning: diffused light, gentle melodies, three children perfectly dressed and waiting angelically in a row to welcome any visitors. Such delightful effects lasted only until the visitors left, when once again the lighting became blinding, the music ceased, the children fought. I have always thought that Chopin should never be incidentally listened to.

When you finally learn to live with what you were given, you get hit by this bodily condition that, sooner or later, women will suffer from: a full, frontal, violent attack without warning, finding us entirely unprepared for the ordeal and causing us untold misery, incapable as we are to defend ourselves against the onslaught; there seems to be a blaze raging both in body and mind as if an invisible enemy had set you on fire; interest is lost on so many fronts, mainly relating to physical intimacy; what is worse is that there is no chance of a cessation of hostilities and these unwarranted attacks will continue, albeit sporadically, into your old age. Yet despite the fighting, we maintain throughout a policy of no surrender, and we carry on as if impervious to attacks. Using militaristic terms to describe the whole experience of the menopause is done on purpose, as it is a stage in our lives that can only be described as war.

In times of despair, I try to remember the line from the only film Trumbo directed: "Use your head!"

I would like to see a shrink; I do not know who I am or what I am doing here; I used to live in a country where I was free, and now I am in a country where I am not free one bit. I said all these things to Mother, and she replied to the adolescent version of myself: What are the neighbours going to think when they find out that a daughter of mine has to see a psychiatrist. *"¿Qué va a pensar la gente? ¿Que van a decir los vecinos?"* And this time, after having listened to her repeating so many times what people and neighbours would think of me, I retorted: *"¡Y a mí qué me importa lo que piense la gente!"* Mother was so terribly shocked by my reply that she did not speak to me for a whole week. It was the first time I had answered back, and it would be the last time, because after that I gave in on everything.

How inadequate I used to feel for not finding the G-sport after searching endlessly. Even a shrink I once dated tried hard to find it. One day, after much trying he suddenly shouted "Eureka!" more for his success than for my pleasure. Did I feel anything different after the discovery, is the question to ask. Certainly not. Any erectile tissue in the area is in fact the clitoris, which has long ramifications and bulbous-like parts. Certain engorged bulbs from an aroused clitoris can be felt through the vaginal wall, and that is precisely what might account for the much talked about G-spot. For decades, women felt inadequate for not finding the illusory spot within their bodies; and in the meantime, someone was getting a few honours for making yet another fictitious discovery at our expense.

For you are, deep down, this very fragile child.

Some of the outlandish people you encounter and befriend (without any logical explanation on your part) can completely obliterate you: he almost persuaded me to get pregnant again claiming that it would be, of all things, the Second Coming.

Mother would regularly say that she did not like repeating things more than once when it came to scolding us if we misbehaved. Her rule was simple: if we disobeyed, she would tell us off and did not expect us to disobey again. *"¡Una vez ha de bastar!"* On my part, I may have extrapolated this maternal command to my romantic relationships. I am left unemotional and unimpressed when told things like my embrace comes at the wrong time or that my sexy move is cheap or that I am getting unnecessarily emotional. I am sorry to say that I give no second chances.

I am now considered to be a stroke survivor in official terms. The stroke bit is not as imposing as having been officially recognised as a survivor.

As a young child I learnt English both intuitively and academically at the same time. Regarding Spanish, I learnt it intuitively from birth; I did not speak it much for several years, by which time it had become a passive language; and then I had to re-learn it as a teenager, but this time academically. Mine was what they call sequential bilingualism. However, all such technicalities are without relevance. The important question to ask is whether you are the same person when you speak a particular language as when you speak another. Or even better: are you two people at the same time? Part of me would be inclined to say "No way!" and part of me would definitely proclaim in a very loud and penetrating voice *"¡Sí, sí, sí!"*

Everyone specialises in their own particular branding. She accuses and he assumes. He assumes that she will invariably like what he likes regardless of her tastes or opinions. And she accuses him of having tastes and opinions that are very different from hers, as if it were his fault.

It was sex by numbers; sex as in a carefully planned military operation; sex as in scientific research, testing and analysing; sex as if carefully dissecting some kind of creature, making sure each section was perfectly preserved although dead. Touching here because this generated a particular reaction, licking there because it produced that other effect. Blowing, bellowing, sucking, chewing, gnawing, chomping, squashing, even pushing. No, this was not the time to discuss what you both wanted. The time was either before the event, or during the relevant *post-mortem*, but not then. Then you were far too busy wondering how on earth you would explain that the whole thing was not really that breathtaking.

The reader might sporadically have to fill in a few gaps in the story.

My Chinese rosewood figure of a fisherman: without a rod, his right hand is curved holding nothing but air, and yet from his eyes you can tell that he lives in the hope of catching as many fish as he can today.

I tried hard at being a good mother, but I admit I probably failed. I learnt it in the traditional way, as was demanded in those days: playing with dolls and dollhouses, pretending to cook and iron with lesser versions of real appliances, trying my best to be tidy and hygienic with everything around me. But it was a kind of sentimental training more than anything, with no one teaching me the serious technicalities of the whole process, the fine detail, the demands, and the exertions. Yes, especially the exertions and the pain.

"La voz de oro de la bebecé" as I was kindly described by one of our regular listeners.

This is what happened during the war: Father had to defend a position at the top of a hill in Northern Spain. It was a strategic post, vital for the battle raging around them. A bird's nest. All the men alongside him had either been wounded or killed, even the commander was seriously injured. And high on that hill, Father would go round and round on all fours, facing the surrounding enemy down below, and firing from the guns placed every few meters on the hilltop by carefully removing the hands and fingers of his dead or injured comrades from the trigger. No, this is not a Gary Cooper movie, but a true and tragic story. Thus, the hill was defended, the enemy retreated, and the battle was won. When the war ended, after endless reports were completed and inquiries into the event rendered, Father received his much-coveted medal. Tragically though, his remarkable courage would not be taken into account when he was wrongly accused of a crime, as we shall see.

And suddenly one day, you will wake up and announce to the world: "I am back!"

It is so easy to admit all your sins and faults to someone who cannot grasp who I am; yes, that professional confessor on the other side of a grid under a veil of darkness. Just in case, I cover my tracks: I am speaking in an unrecognizable voice, changing the rhythm of my speech, using very different words from my usual ones so that I cannot be identified, telling all with a softness and innocence that have already exonerated me from any transgression that I might hasten to come clean with. And then I leave the confessionary, feeling on top of the world because my offences have been factually erased from the universe.

A WOMAN ALONE

When Grandfather learnt that his second child was another daughter, he left the family home in a rage and wandered along the streets of the city for several days.

Until I got the hang of Spanish, I would sign all my letters with the adverb *amorosamente*.

Luck would have it that I ended up in a whorehouse of a place. Not much difference between selling flesh for money and trading in these three: my precious time, my grey cells and my dream to be free. Such items are peddled in the workplace for a meagre amount. Does it mean that for a higher price you should sell all you are, throwing in your soul as well? Eventually it all comes to a grand finale, since life travels so very fast: you are still undecided whether to leave or not, but in the end the decision is taken for you because it is time to go. And go you will with your hard-earned pension, to live out the last stretch of your life outside those walls. Had I seen for myself what it all boiled down to, I would not have got caught up in the fallacy of a stable job.

She decides to go for it on her own. It is so very easy: she thinks of something nice, and her mind does it all for her. Any scene will do, in a restaurant, on board a train, in the middle of the desert. Yes, I arrive on a gently trotting camel, or I travel on board a noisy and quivering carriage, or I am served mouth-watering food that I have never tasted before. It is so stress-free to do it thus: no catching strange diseases here, no pregnancies, no apologising for not getting it quite right, no asking *"How was it for you?"* whilst predictably sucking on an untipped cigarette. Certainly, no expectations unfulfilled. To the point. Waves, agitation, a plateau of distension, and if you wish you can do it immediately again from scratch. And once again, and again, and certainly again. And you, no one else, decides when it is all over, when it starts, when it is interrupted, when it comes to a temporary halt. Fleeting, ungraspable pleasure, unshared and selfish, lonely and inaccessible. And yet I keep thinking that the world should be shared, surely there is more beauty when it is seen by four luminous eyes than by only two. Is there not?

I wanted everything to happen quickly: children to grow up, responsibilities to end, holidays to arrive, a season to change into the next season. And after this manic race, here I am, so much out of breath.

Mother taught me there were things that had to be kept secret at any cost: age, income or lack of it, family feuds, love affairs, religious beliefs, medical issues, the most private thoughts and, especially, any sad events in one's life. Until the day I discovered that I could write a memoir, I closely followed her advice.

A rigorous work ethic and a stark morality, all strictly Catholic, governed my formative years. They still do, but now without the flourish.

Oh, how many times have I done this, whether in real life or in dreams: I get up from my seat as my name is announced. I walk up to the makeshift stage, and either recite from memory or read my poem or my story from a script. Although it is a smallish audience, in my mind it feels like one huge creature ready to gorge on me if I am not good enough. I must entertain those spectators for a few minutes, allow them a happy break from their harsh and uneventful day. Initially I would complain and talk about my grievances in front of them, whether I delivered poetry or prose. But with time I learnt to amuse the audience, tell them imaginary tales that were unrelated to my own petty life, and engage with them almost intimately. In the end, we have much in common the audience and I, all of us on the same one-way inexplicable journey. The final applause is but an added bonus.

We must give each one their dues. He adored me, physically, emotionally, cerebrally. Being an artist and an aesthete, he praised all I had: my hands and feet as icons of some obscure religion of which he was undoubtedly the highest priest; my intimate spaces as a territory to incessantly and excitedly explore; my eyes and mouth as gates to a new world, perhaps even a magical one. He would talk about my body as if a work of art, he would compliment my mind with passion and intensity, he would venerate me as if I were nothing less than a saint. But on all other counts, he was shit.

Had I been able to put my grievances to Mother, would she have admitted her mistakes and oversights that shaped or misshaped my character? Instead of all that, I am sure that she would have simply replied: *"Dadas las circunstancias, hija mía, esto es lo único que pude hacer."*

I can see and smell the sea right now, on command, as if I were right there on the coast, exactly where the waves break. What astonishing recollections the sea arouses, engraved forever in me. They are almost the same sea, the one in my mind and the one for real. In full bloom in August. Water of the deepest and darkest colour, with just a handful of white horses. The tranquil sound of waves gradually rising. A tiny fishing vessel on the horizon. My desire to be alone there, and yet wanting to hold someone's hand to walk along the beach. The weather as warm and breezy as it used to be. Yes, in my memory the sea appears with the same shade of blue, and I beautify it with the touch and the smell of seawater that I remember so vividly. But there is one thing that I cannot get quite right in my mind: my imaginary sea cannot wash away my troubles as the real sea used to do back then, that is for sure.

At the end of the day, I am not necessarily an authority on the subject of my life.

In standard relationships you are given to choose between acquaintance, friendship, love or passion. But there are a few other in-between modes, at times so much more comforting. Comradeship, for example. Amity, for example. Harmony, for example.

And so here are two versions of the same story, one in English and the other Spanish. Alike but not the same, and not two viewpoints but two different emotional realities, one is 'Zero Negative' and the other is *'Cero negativo'*: I could tell from his stunted fingers that he was partial to all material things, from his short nose that he was not a man of character, from his eyes flickering as if assessing the odds that he was a gambler, from his clean-cut suit that he was most definitely an accountant. In none of my forebodings (I prefer that term to feminine intuition, which is what my editor infuriatingly calls my speculative nature) was I wrong. He revealed, in later conversations, that he loved to place bets, and in fact would place bets at any time and on anything. He also said that he was an accountant for several small firms, and that he worked from home. And although he found it difficult to look at me in the eye, which is what usually happens with the miserable at heart, when he spoke about his favourite subjects –cards, dice, horses, greyhounds – his eyes would sparkle like gems. "The perfect man to commit a murder on my behalf!" I said to myself. *Por las manos de dedos cortos supe que le gustaban las riquezas materiales, por la nariz chata que era hombre de poco carácter, por la mirada perdida que era soñador pero sólo en el juego, por el cuerpo enjuto que era contable. En ninguno de mis presentimientos (prefiero ese término al de intuición femenina que tanto usa mi editor cuando me pongo a especular) me equivoqué porque me fue revelado, en nuestros posteriores diálogos, que efectivamente le gustaban el juego y las apuestas, apostaba en cualquier momento y por cualquier cosa; que por profesión se dedicaba a la contabilidad de varias empresas pequeñas y que trabajaba desde casa. Y si habitualmente le costaba mirar a los ojos como le sucedería a cualquier ser desdichado, cuando hablaba de sus temas predilectos – cartas, dados, caballos, galgos– le chispeaba la expresión como el sediento que descubre un oasis. He aquí, me dije, un hombre perfecto para pedirle que cometa un asesinato en mi nombre.*

The police get too close, and the student demonstration breaks up, dispersed as we are by men on horseback. It is late in the evening, and I run for it, but I am no athlete. A mounted policeman catches up with me in seconds. I can smell the horse, hear the man clenching his teeth. He has a truncheon in one hand, a pistol in his sling. The horse pulls back when climbing a small hill and I manage to overtake it. The policeman uses foul, explicitly sexual language. He has been trained to inflict maximum damage and leave no traces. But I have not been trained for this. No, I go to university and return home in the evening. I attend demonstrations to assert that I do not agree. I dream about going back to

London, and never coming back to this fascist regime. Political parties try to woo me in class, but I limit my insurrection to putting things on paper, confident that poetry is the most effective form of protest. At the scene of the demonstration, the mounted policeman and I finally come to a road with lots of traffic. It might be the end of me, but there will be witnesses to the event: an agent on horseback beating up a young female student near the district of *Moncloa*, they would claim; she died from the fall, a victim of pounding with a truncheon, under the horse's hoofs, with a policeman deafeningly shouting abuse. But with the dictatorship in its last throes, they do not want to generate further bad publicity. The papers might just pick up the story, and it would definitely not read like fucking poetry. Some things just cannot be hushed, even by vicious dictators; not everyone has sold their soul to the thugs running the country. And then the guy on horseback says something: *"¡Es culpa tuya, puta!"* His truncheon shines in the moonlight, and the bright light seems to make him rethink: he has much to gain personally but far too much to lose jobwise, and so he pulls on the reins, making the horse halt and turn around. I am then left solely to my luck. I run faster than I have ever run, will ever run. And on the main road, a Peugeot stops with three students inside. Is this *déjà vu*? I get in and tell them that, one day soon, I will leave the country and try to reinvent myself elsewhere. They seem to agree with every word I say, if only to pacify me. But what does anyone know about anyone?

It is not that these terrible people who rule the world did not grow up –the problem is that they did.

Between English school and Spanish school, both single-sex and run by nuns, I was taken for a very short while to a small school in Madrid, a so-called *academia*, with a huge mix of kids. It was so different from girls-only English school. I was shocked when a couple of boys were viciously slapped several times by a most sadistic teacher in front of the class for not having done their Geography homework. I would feel so terribly sorry for those boys, who were otherwise charming and funny, especially one of them who was particularly good-looking and sweet. Later on, I learnt that this particular teacher was a civil guard moonlighting as an educator, and he most probably believed that he had the authority to do anything he wanted to young students without fear of reprisal. No, no one who sucked up to that callous regime was reprimanded.

He is obviously in awe of her enigmatic smile and her even more cryptic silence. And then, raising his voice a full octave, he says: "Oh this is so lovely! I love the way you do that to me! Do not stop, go on! Oh, oh, oh!" Imitating the female voice is difficult enough, yet his attempt to emulate hers is not so unconvincing. He has kindly written a script for her in view of her silence towards the sexual actions he has just performed; and even more kindly, he has enunciated the script. When stereotypes enter, individuality exits.

Lake Constance, a boat taking me from one country to the next, persistent showers, the air reeking of rotting greenery, excited travellers on board shouting in order to be heard above the noise of the engine. I must write a story based on this place, this boat, these characters, under such a dire grey sky. The subject? Even though I travelled to Lake Constance to inject more life into my soul, the subject of my story would be quite the opposite, for all the elements around me were crying out for it: the story would be about a woman going to the lake solely in search of death but, by a strange twist of the plot, after several attempts at ending it all she was still alive. Someone or something always seemed to prevent her from killing herself, whether it was the warm weather, the gentle ripples on the surface of the lake, a kind word by a stranger. This story was never written, but it still swims in my mind.

"Did you see dinosaurs when you were a child, Mother?"

In the case of people who are not damaged goods –but have led a so-called normal life, with a regular family upbringing where parents are proud of their children, children look up to their parents, siblings are loved, grandparents visit on Sundays, Christmas is one huge happy family occasion, extended family means emotional nourishment and support, and all is well– for each and every one of these well-adjusted, well-to-do and worthy citizens, a piece of damaged goods comes as a complete shock. And when at the Old Girls' Reunion, D asked me about my family life and I told her about Mother's illness and death, Father's illness and death, divorce and other glum circumstances and various kinds of dysfunctionality, she looked at me with a mixture of disbelief and disgust, for I was spoiled goods, damaged, seconds, flawed, unloved and unwanted. Her almost impenetrable gaze said it all: with a woman like her in my proximity, the world as we know it could well end for those of us who are not damaged goods in any way whatsoever; and my hard-earned stability, which comes from centuries of might and dominance, will be put seriously at risk and all will be lost. She replied not a thing to me and simply walked away, only for her to suffer a similar fate to Mother's the following year, leaving behind her five young children and a very disturbed husband.

'Manual de Urbanidad': Mother purchased the book for me and made me memorise its rules; she asked questions about what the book said, and I had to provide answers; she would comment on what I did or did not do right in certain social situations, and whether my actions followed the teachings in the book or opposed them. The word 'civility' is the closest to *urbanidad*, but I have always wondered whether this sort of thing can be taught theoretically in a book, instead of learning it the hard way in real life, by imitation or, even better, by avoidance.

"Arzobispado de Madrid-Alcalá," Father would reply when answering the phone. Most callers hung up when they heard such words, thinking that they had dialled the wrong number and were in fact speaking to religious authorities. Other callers remained silent, unsure of whether to take it seriously or to burst out laughing. And then Father would put the phone down, a wry smile on his face until the next phone call.

I once interviewed the famous tenor F for my Arts programme. As well as working as a broadcaster, I was studying *bel canto* at the time, and he and I discussed my musical progress. He invited me to go and sing for him in his hotel. "Call my secretary to arrange an appointment. I have a piano in my hotel room. You will sing and I will play the piano for you." I thanked him and left. There are photographs to prove that I interviewed him, but there is nothing to prove that I most certainly did not go to his hotel room. When I told my singing teacher about F's proposition, she said that he had also approached her years earlier, after a concert in which they had both sung. Years later, the press reported what had been well known in operatic circles for decades, as many women began to gradually come forward:

all that time, he had been nothing less than a voracious sexual predator, taking advantage of young female singers and assaulting them. Even in the mellifluous musical world, a woman's testimony is up against a wall of silence.

Is she not part of the cosmos, perhaps even the cosmos itself?

You can take someone out of a dictatorship, but you can never take away the effects of a dictatorship that were etched in blood.

Her life is finally hers and no longer shared freely among so many.

A kind of folly starts to show its head at the age of thirteen when the body is acquiring a distinct womanly shape. I would shower with my swimming suit on, I confess. It was all perfectly reasonable at the time: I did so in case a fire was declared in the house and firefighters had to make their way through the bathroom. In such a guise, they would see me not as a naked girl, but as someone who was getting ready to go for a swim. Yes, laugh all you wish, but embarrassment around nudity had been drilled into me. Or perhaps there was another truth to this story: I wanted to prevent myself from seeing who I was developing into.

The strength of my feelings towards EFG could only be a sign that there was something formidable between us. I could sense his feelings too, and almost by accident he said that there were two women in his life, referring to his wife and to me. I remember that whenever he approached me in the office corridor, the air preceding him would stir my body and my mind in intense waves, almost making me lose my balance. When one day I had the courage to declare my love to him, he rejected me by saying *"Estoy infinitamente enamorado de mi mujer."* There is no way you can fight against the word *infinitamente*, it has a sense of the final and, worse, the impossible. And then he added, in a very clear voice, that we would be together one day, not in this life but in another life: *"Estaremos juntos en otra vida..."* Such a statement makes me want to believe desperately in an afterlife, although everything around me points to the fact that it cannot conceivably exist. Even the possibility of a love affair with EFG in another life will not make me change my mind.

I wrote a novella equating my old workplace to something not very nice. It was not so much a mildly concealed metaphor as a direct comparison, easy to understand by all, whether observers or perpetrators: co-workers were fiends, corruption was rife, animosity and malevolence were the main features of the whole place. As expected, the novella was called 'Hell'.

It is as if she were several women at the same time, each one needing to be appeased with the appropriate diet of events and attributes: the conventional bourgeois who enjoys a life of style; the unconventional artist who wishes nothing but to break with tradition; the radical individual who aims to deconstruct all that is wrong with the world; the child who is still playing with fire at this age. Since all these characters are real to some degree (namely, none are deceptions), what we must ask is which one is the most accurate and which one the least genuine, and more importantly: which one of them will prevail or are they all cursed to forever live side by side?

In Madrid I used to teach English as a young student, something that I truly loved and which allowed me to keep the language alive within me. Initially I taught my schoolfriends; later on, I was a teacher at my own school when the English teacher was sick; and then I taught privately, and most of my pupils were much older than me. Inexplicably, I always learnt more than I taught, as if I was the main beneficiary of my teaching.

The first time I thought God existed was on a Good Friday when the sky was lit with a dull and yellow light, just like it would have been in the valley of Gethsemane. I was sure that the sullen sky was the irrefutable proof that God did exist and that the whole world was crying for the death of Jesus Christ. I was eight years old and had yet to come to grips with meteorology

My biggest turn-on? More than exquisite manners and no four-letter words, it is living life ever so passionately.

An unforgivable act: a 19th century illustrated edition of The Thousand and One Nights, given to me by Grandfather as a gift from his library, mysteriously disappeared from my bookshelves. I thought of various options, even the impossible: theft, fire, magic. It turned out to be a much simpler explanation: Father had come to the conclusion that a fourteen-year-old should not be reading books that he thought were blatant obscenities. The book did not end up in Father's own library but in the rubbish bin outside the house; by the time I realised what had happened, it was too late to find the book among the piles of garbage. As always, the usual contradictions about Father: a man who was an intensely creative spirit at heart, downright defeated by his blinkered and pathetic upbringing.

Grandparents never liked Father one bit. They very much lamented that their eldest and most precious daughter had chosen someone from the winning side in the war, for they had not only been geographically republican but, more importantly, ideologically republicans. To make matters worse, when Mother married, she had to give up her highly prized job, which meant that her salary would no longer supplement her parents' inadequate income. Father once dared to comment on this fact and was immediately thrown out of his future in-law's house by Mother's younger brother. The animosity between Father and his in-laws continued once he and Mother were married, and it became a constant throughout our lives. As a child I witnessed several decidedly unpleasant scenes that impacted strongly on me. There was nothing physical, but mostly verbal; no shouting, mainly murmuring and a constant aversion towards the other party. It is difficult enough to have a relationship with someone we are in love with, but whose idea was it that we had to get along with their families as well.

Perhaps she should write using fewer words and more blank spaces.

I would gladly give up my hopelessness for an iota of persuasive evidence that there exists another world after this one.

Even though nobody had explained a thing about how it all worked, she somehow managed to pick it up as she went along.

She uses both intuition and perception. She writes stream of consciousness sometimes, and then revises heavily. Or she writes with solely logic as tool, and then allows herself to get carried away in a more spontaneous fashion. Sometimes her first draft is acceptable, but other times she is still struggling after a hundred drafts. There is no single way to write, and likewise there is no secret to writing. It is a blend of many features, some of them contradictory: experience, having been around the block many times; intuition and, chiefly, instinct; a good dose of rationality and, if you can manage it, level-headedness; the ability and humility to revise endlessly until you tame the wild creature of your writing; and last but certainly not least, brief bouts of insanity, because no one in their right mind would embark on such a hazardous voyage.

As my breasts were developing, I told no one. But Mother came to me one day with one of her brassieres and said that she would tuck it here and pin it there, and that I would quickly have a bra in my size. She went off with her sewing implements and within an hour, the bra became several sizes smaller. I, a mere child, could not possibly fill her space. She would always be the greater woman in every sense.

There was a time in my late teens when I unconditionally abhorred consumerism, mostly products like make-up. And yet I really loved colouring my lips, there was something fascinating about lipstick that made you look like a character from a fairy tale. So, believe it or not, in my bag I would carry, yes, a beetroot inside a small plastic bag with a tiny penknife; I would cut into the beetroot with the penknife, extracting the juice and dabbing my lips with that most gorgeous colour. No knives are allowed any more, and so nowadays what I carry with me in my bag is a lipstick of the brightest orange shade and from an excellent and extremely expensive brand.

A WOMAN ALONE

Perhaps there was no need to dwell on those sad days after all.

For those of us who feel we have no country, Virginia Woolf said this: "As a woman my country is the whole world..."

Decades ago, I was raised to be the perfect female whether I wanted it or not, and so I was taught embroidery, crochet, needlepoint, sewing, patternmaking, tailoring, among many other endeavours. Yes, all those things that were not really transferable to my situation as a hard-working wordsmith in this day and age. But we need to ask ourselves whether, at this time of doom, might all these vanished and ancient skills be useful once again in a world where nothing will be done for us anymore?

Is your life also non-linear?

As far as we know –but then we know so very little– the universe is incapable of visualising or even imagining itself: it cannot hear its roaring sounds, nor admire its vibrant colours, nor envision its improbable dimensions nor feel its pulsating existence. It could well be then that, when you disappear from the face of this planet, the visible and audible and sentient universe disappears not only *for* you but *with* you.

Wednesday's child is full of woe.

Pain will always be there, but suffering is up to her.

No, there is no plan B.

A WOMAN ALONE

It is so very easy: walking in the park and nothing else. All those steps, count them; they peak to ten thousand a day, while I am being utterly mindful of what I am doing. And even though my imprints are of no consequence and will leave no mark, I am duly aware of each and every one of my steps without fail. I was there and I was then, I will decisively state.

What Borges said was ultimately an explanation: *"... lo que era todo tiene que ser nada..."*

The great love of my life, to whom I dedicated a book of short stories that was encouragingly praised by critics, never once slept with me.

Given Father's background (his mother dying when he was very young, his artistic career being cut short, his taking part in the war as a teenage soldier, his regressive ideas about women, and his blind belief in the gifts that religion had to offer), he did not know what to do with emotions and would always call out for discipline, mostly his own. Thus, when Mother was dying, he told me that on her deathbed she had enquired about my siblings. Did she enquire about me, I asked. And he plainly said no, without giving me further details. I was taken back, so very saddened but trying not to show it. I then remarked that she was not getting any better in hospital and asked about what her illness really was. Father kept quiet and lowered his eyes. And then I knew that whatever afflicted Mother, it was deadly; and I started to cry desperately, even scream. And all that time Father just stood there, as firm as a soldier, with an infinitesimal smile on his lips because he could not think of a single thing to say in the face of adversity.

When for a second you stop breathing at the end of the exhale and before you embark on a new inhale, the World stops with you.

I am now walking for all the driving I did over the years.

I do not consider eternity a gift, unless you get answers to the usual questions: eternity doing what, interacting with whom.

She equipped herself with enough stuff –books, music and mementoes– to last centuries and yet here she is without having read or listened to or cherished all of these things, now in the last third of her life.

Yes, even now she is a work in progress.

I was invited to a conference on translation; and then we were invited to a rather lavish dinner. At the end came the turn of after-dinner speeches. Goodness, I was asked to speak without prior warning. I had a mild panic attack and yet delivered what I could, but it was a tough situation to be put in. The guy before me had boasted about the thousands of pages he had translated in the course of his professional life, so how can you follow that up but by being utterly alarmed because of your age and immaturity. Happily I came out of it almost unscathed, yet what was going on inside my mind was so much worse than the vulnerability that people saw. And then time passed, as it does, and the size of your achievements does not matter in any field whatsoever, but only the effort of the endeavour will count. In any case, by now I have the reached tens of thousands of pages as a translator.

The only good thing about perfection is that it cannot be surpassed.

I decided that, from then on, I would follow the flow and let life lead me; she was wise enough.

On the one hand, there is the worrying style of life; and on the other, there is the perilous way of life. Can they ever be reconciled, we ask each other.

I became a hoarder and refused to part with anything; it was my way of holding on to the past. Initially, hoarding was about bits of paper; but later on, it meant all those interminable e-files with unfinished business, the cut-outs that remain once a life is over. In a way, you could say a memoir is nothing but the hoarding of all those things which would otherwise have to be discarded, as all things will be in the end.

There is possibly a type of grace that comes from having lived.

Perhaps other memories could have been selected for this memoir, but those included here are the ones that did not completely obliterate me.

We tend to show such terrible animosity towards cruel luck or impending death, but then it is nobody's fault.

It was not that life proved to be too short or too fast, but that I was running through it like a madwoman.

To call it literary fiction sounds far too precious. To call it popular fiction seems to dilute the whole text into a lesser category. I suppose we must navigate between genres and take the best of each one, steering safely under propitious winds, if any, until you come into sight of the elusive land of some kind of story.

Eduardo Embry: *"Mi amor es una manzana caída de la memoria."*

She endured, even when wasting away at the edges.

Paraphrasing Simone de Beauvoir: Why impose limits by saying you are this and not that, or you prefer this and not the other, when the ideal is about loving a human being without feeling fear or restraint or obligation.

This is not just lipstick –it is war paint.

Penny Black, Penny Blue, Penny Red: my stamp collection stopped expanding the day I realised that I could not have all the stamps in the world.

I tried hard with a piano, with a guitar, and even with my own voice. But nothing came of it. Music always seemed to be beyond my reach; words have always been second best.

Mother said that what remains, after all is said and done, is something called *poso*, referring to the stuff that floats to the top of wine, when well-aged. Better known as the flower, or *velo de flor*, it is a yeast that gives the wine its distinct flavour, prevents excessive oxygenation and provides nutrients. It can sometimes ruin certain wines, but with others it is very much sought after, notably with sherry. And after all these years, Mother was proved right: in the end, all that lingers is a fine and innocuous film over and above memories, preserving them from too much oxygenation and the effects of the real world, yet giving them a mild flavour reminding us faintly of the done and dusted past.

"O frabjous day!" I would reply when someone wept in front of me, quoting Carroll.

Sex is so very personal that perhaps one should hand a potential partner a flyer with all the do's and the don'ts so they get some of it right, or at least they do not get all of it wrong.

The unpredictability of life should be soothing you instead of hurting you, and that is because the terrible things you suspect will happen may in fact not happen at all.

I am sorry to spoil your idea of fun, but sex is definitely overrated.

Strangely I do not feel exposed in this book.

After certain episodes I needed to mother myself: pamper and treat and spoil myself. This has put me in risky situations, mostly in financial terms. But mothering became something that I also kindly did for others. So many wanted me to mother them: sharing their most private thoughts and grievances with me, whinging and whining, seeking solace and support, hoping that I would get them out of scrapes and save them from any evils thrown their way. I willingly mothered so many, and for so long, that in due course it became less of a caring and generous act on my part and more of a deeply emotional and merciless wear and tear on my soul.

I loved it when he said that my surnames meant 'River of Salvation'.

You have to find out what you really want to do with your life, someone daringly said to me, as if it were that easy.

A new day has just started, and I am not yet ready for it.

I used to attend a group meeting once a month. We were all parents of grown-up children with mental health issues. After attending several sessions, I still could not tell whether it was Nature or Nurture to blame. This was discussed at length: was it the parent's fault or the fault of Evolution and its many attempts to get things right over millennia. In the end, whatever the evidence, no one can convince parents that their child's issues are not entirely their fault and solely their problem.

As if life were not mine to keep.

In trying to pigeonhole me, he left most of who I was out of the picture.

As folk tales go, this viral horror will last a thousand days. But that is another story.

Look at the toy dragon on your desk, the bee, the sheep, the rabbit, the cow; suck a mint sweet or two; sharpen a pencil; listen to Schubert's Ave Maria sung by Victoria de los Ángeles; try to sound less official in intimate moments; avoid obsessing with what has disappeared forever or is not yet here; think for once that at this age you may have no role to play any longer, however well prepared you are.

All these family members might be right in that I am cannibalising my own life.

If you believe that it is all happening on cue, you immediately start feeling better.

Paraphrasing Norma Kamali: The real revolution on how we use words and how we write is about to arrive, and I don't know whether we should be afraid or not.

Tie up any loose ends: it would be silly to trip during your final sprint.

Jorge Manrique: *"Nuestras vidas son los ríos que van a dar a la mar, que es el morir."* When writing equals the truth, it cannot be surpassed.

To my disadvantage, I was led to believe by my family that I was precocious, a real smarty pants. I was soon cut down to size by the real superheroines that I met in my life.

Is she better at writing than living, or the other way round? Whatever the answer, it does not mean that she is a prodigious writer or a terrible liver. She can more or less manage both, in varying degrees, with different commitments, at changing speeds, in various guises.

Revisiting Shirley Jackson: In the country of the story the writer is queen.

A WOMAN ALONE

I do not love in the manner I like to love nor in the manner I know I can love.

It is always about war, is it not: Mother lived a war; I, her daughter, lived a post-war era; you, my daughters, live a different war, its insidious presence in most of what you must go through and its imperceptible assaults on the many fronts you are trying to defend.

There comes a day in a writer's life when words take over and every sentence appears on the page as if by accident.

Eleanor Roosevelt said something like happiness is a by-product. A by-product of what, she did not specify.

Oh, the untranslatable tango by Gardel and Le Pera: "*Sueño con el pasado que añoro / Y el tiempo viejo que lloro / Y que nunca volverá…*"

If you think that gone are the days when we could walk freely and embrace everyone and do anything, then remember that even without a virus not everybody in every country can walk freely or embrace those they love or do everything they wish.

I am by no means an expert, a theoretician, an academic, a historian. Merely a practising storyteller, though I can never get to practise enough.

How surreptitious all this superfluous pondering about endless options and possibilities –from the wings, such ideas enter unnoticed until they fully occupy centre stage and take over the play of her life.

Time can be fast, but at this stage in my life it is mostly reckless.

I can honestly claim that X was, put simply, a very bad man. He was the one who raped me. Yes, you can call it statutory rape. Without penetration, is it still rape? Yes, in my view it is still rape. But you may call it sexual assault if you prefer, most do. With penetration it is a colossal crime, but without penetration it cannot possibly be a lesser one. And that is because I was debased, torn, rubbished. There was desecration, carnal familiarity against my will, aggression, use of force, assault, invasion of my most secluded and private space. So, there you are, rape without penetration can only be rape. And no, I will not give you his full name because you would easily recognise him. He was a colleague at work, and I was young. He lived close by, and I went to his apartment to return a book. The moment I arrived he propelled himself on me and tried to take my dress off, placing his hands firmly on buttocks and breasts. I defended myself as I could, but he was rough. Rough is perhaps not the right word, uncivilized is better. Vile is even more adequate. We fought, I screamed. And suddenly, the assault stopped. What? Yes, his premature ejaculation was my luck; whether it happened because of a sexual dysfunction or because of his nauseating excitement, who would want to know. One touch of the flesh and it all poured out, with a large stain appearing on his trousers. He was in love with me, he claimed in an embarrassed whimper, but did not know how to express it other than by assaulting me. And as he let go of my wrists, I jumped onto the floor, pulled up my dress and ran out of the place as fast as I possibly could. I thought he would stop me from leaving his flat, and perhaps even get violent, but he did not move an inch. He looked entirely pitiable lying on an armchair, yet without inducing any sense of pity in me but only repulsion. No, I would not forget and certainly not forgive. I should have accused him of assault and violation, but had no proof, no witnesses. If they had examined me, I would have been intact, and he would have denied an assault ever took place, especially after putting his trousers in the wash. What could I do, I asked myself the next day. I decided to take justice into my own hands, entirely in public. At the canteen at work, he sat at the table with a tray holding a glass of wine and a plate with a freshly fried steak. I took the glass and poured the wine over the steak, as much of an outpour as his shameful ejaculation had been. The red wine drowned the meat on his plate, an island in the middle of a midnight sea. Everyone around us probably understood. I remained the unbroken, the intact, the untouched, the superior woman. Yet I should have denounced him to HR and taken him to court. But it happened such a long time ago that I am sure that if I had said anything to those in authority the incident would have been swept under the carpet, as was done in both large and small corporations. Had it occurred today, there are so many things a woman can do if faced with such a horrid ordeal. I could have threatened him with exposure and taken pictures on my iPhone. Censured him in various chat groups. Sought refuge in sexual assault helplines. Instagrammed selfies of my dishevelled state and the stains on his trousers. Ranted on YouTube about the shock and the humiliation I was subjected to. Tweeted that he raped me without penetration, but this was solely because he came far, far too early. Sent private messages to my female friends with minute details of the assault. Punished him graphically on Flickr. Created a Facebook page about the despicable monster. Declared him a professional outcast on LinkedIn. Organised an event on the subject of rape crowdfunded by Indiegogo. Zoomed, Webbexed, GotoMeetinged, Kudoed, Teamed. Yes, I could go on. Even in times of lockdown, there are just so many outlets to support you in your fight for justice. No, nowadays we are not alone. As it was back then, the incident remains unresolved to this day. This was yet another very, very, very cold case in the history of the plight of women.

Not the brightest and not made in the image of any superior being, but just bungling, thoroughly puerile, easily duped, attracted to the blatantly trivial, fatuous to a fault. Do you recognise this species?

The last time I unreservedly wept was when watching a film in which the role of the protagonist was played by Óscar Martínez.

Do you choose your words for how they sound rather than for what they mean?

Someone, but who knows who it was, said that there is no such thing as writing only rewriting. But on her part, she would say that there is nothing like writing except reading; without reading, writing would never be possible.

When I grew up and learnt that Father had fought for the wrong side in the war, I was unable to speak for a week: it turned out that I was the offspring of one of the victors, a soldier who battled for the enemy. It was shocking and painful to know the truth; I was ashamed and bewildered. And yet how things can change. In time, the tables were turned, and I would become the child of a victim. Father was ultimately oppressed and humiliated by the same repressive regime that he had fought for as a very young and inexperienced man, as we shall see.

The high school in Madrid was a girls-only establishment. We sat in rows, one girl behind the other, up to ten girls in each row; and then the next row and the next, up to five rows. Yes, we were lots of girls in our class, and we were not placed in random order but rigorously classified. The first row from front to back would include the girls with the best monthly grades, all the way to the girl with the worst grades sitting at the back of the very last row. So, there we were in the first row, supposedly the clever and privileged ones, with the girls in the last row considered as the worst students. What hideous sense of entitlement we had on that first row; what unkindness was instilled into us by this pigeonholing according to ability. Any such feelings of superiority soon evaporated when we eventually moved to mixed colleges for our foundation course before attending university. Away from our familiar and discriminatory settings we felt lost, surrounded by kids from all backgrounds, without any type of classification or division or discrimination. Never again would we be allocated a special place on account of our grades, not during the foundation course and certainly not later at university. We soon adapted and saw the old system of classifying as shameful and bigoted. However, there was one thing that we missed from that classifying of girls in rows. And it had nothing to do with academic prowess or the lack of it. It was about playing with the hair of the girl sitting in front of you; you see, in those endless rows, the desks were very close with one narrowly behind the other. Of course, you had to ask the girl in front of you for her permission: *"¿Puedo jugar con tu pelo?"* The reply would always be *sí*, and then you plaited the girl's hair, brushed it with your fingers, made little buns, scrunched it, caressed it. Some girls already had pigtails or ponytails, and these would be undone and then redone in a different style. During break in the school yard, we would boast and laugh about our new hairstyles. It was such a pleasurable feeling both to play with someone's hair and to have someone play with your hair. I remember most of us had long hair, in some cases all the way down to our waist, so it was easy to create all sorts of wonderful looks. We did it at lesson-time while being taught by our teachers. No one in a position of authority at school ever said that we could not play with other girls' hair during lessons, and it was considered an entirely innocent game. And yet it was our first contact with a very meek form of eroticism. No, no one thought that teenage girls could have any idea of what lust was, given that the school was a single-sex denominational institution. In my case, being a good student, most of the time I sat in the first desk of that first row. The girl behind me could play with my hair, but I could not play with anyone's hair for there was no one there. Likewise, the last girl in the last row could play with the hair of the girl in front, but no one could play with hers, for there was no one behind her. Many years later, we learnt this particular girl who usually sat at the end of the very last row (in other words, the one that always got the worst marks in the class) was seriously dyslexic, but by then she had missed out on both her education and her potential friendships.

The velvety hue of my African violet.

At work I was appointed head of a woman's group, which in fact turned out to be a precursor of future equalities departments in the workplace. Women flocked to me to complain about cases of sexual harassment. So-and-so puts his hand down my blouse when I am typing; so-and-so gets too close when dictating, breathing into my hair; when passing me in the corridor, so-and-so touches whatever he can get his hands on; so-and-so flashed at me and asked me to perform a fellatio. When I officially complained to a top brass of such misdeeds, he insisted that I give him the names of the victims. I said that I was sworn to secrecy, and that women would not trust me anymore if I divulged who the victims were. "But I can give you the names of the perpetrators, if you wish," to which he did not reply.

And this is her question: *¿Es que con los años he perdido el interés en descifrar enigmas, y ya no me interesan el misterio, el problema sin resolver, la explicación sin dar, las cosas sin hacer?*

Aged 14, I watched '2001, A Space Odyssey' on my own at a Madrid cinema. The Kubrick movie had just been released, and everyone was talking about it as the most ground-breaking event in the history of film. I was supposed to meet up with several friends as we had agreed to watch it together, but at the last minute they decided not to join me; I always thought it was because of pressure from their parents against allowing their children to watch what at the time was seen as an avant-garde and even revolutionary film, but my friends never explained. It was in fact surprising that the film had managed to squeeze through the strict censorship laws of the day. I waited outside the cinema with the ticket in my hand, and at the last minute I went into the theatre and watched the film on my own. I was blown away by what I saw and thought it was beyond anything I had ever seen or imagined. I was so very excited when I got home, and I told my family about how great the film was. To my shock, though, I was severely scolded. What are people going to think about seeing a young girl on her own in the cinema? *"¿Qué va a decir la gente?"*

A female celebrity once said publicly that a woman should be a sex-worker in the bedroom. But I say that, if a woman already has a profession, she should be unwilling to take on board a different profession just to make others feel better.

I really wish that I could have had a much more literary existence because the life I lead looks pretty conventional and unadventurous. But my mind is not one little bit conventional; on the contrary, it is utterly unconventional and unorthodox if you were to get to know me.

The last time I unreservedly wept was when watching a film in which the role of the protagonist was played by Óscar Martínez.

Father was named after an older child in the family. It was a little boy who had tragically died when very young, a few years before Father was born. As a result, Father was given the same first name and would always be compared to the dead child. He was constantly told that his namesake would have done the opposite of what he was doing and would have behaved better than he was behaving and be so much more studious than he was. Father could never fit in the other boy's shoes for the simple reason that the dead boy had never really grown up to wear shoes; that older boy was but a faded memory in the mind of Father's parents. Interestingly, there is a similar story told about Salvador Dalí; he was named after his older brother, who had also died young and well before Dalí was born. What a very tragic way to lead a life: in Father's case, it led him to never be himself; in Dali's case, we all know where it led him to.

I cannot say it more accurately than Fran Landesman: "Don't be ashamed, / everybody's got scars, / from our various wars / on the way to the stars."

When many years ago I interviewed *prima ballerina* Alicia Alonso, I saw for myself that she was made of the silkiest feathers, just like a true swan.

As a teenager in Spain, I had to take three lesser subjects at school: Religion, Gymnastics and the so-called *FEN*, which stood for *'Formación del Espíritu Nacional'*, a subject based on the principles of the fascist ideology on which the Francoist dictatorship was founded. We had to learn by heart endless pages of preposterous ideas meant to indoctrinate our young minds. The principles of the so-called *'democracia orgánica'* of the regime were based not on political parties and free elections but on a parliament occupied by designated representatives of what were considered the three main groupings in society: families, municipalities, and unions. All such representatives were appointed from above and had to be strict followers of the official governing party called *Movimiento Nacional*, or *Movimiento* for short. At school, we had the same energetic teacher for Gym and for *FEN*, and she made us toughly exercise both our bodies and our minds, shaping us into the healthy and obedient followers of the authoritarian regime the country had to endure for many decades. We called those three subjects the three Marys, *las tres Marías*, and you had to pass all three of them, notably *FEN*, if you wanted to move to the next year up. Thus, those three dreary and dreaded subjects covered the all-important areas of young people's education at the time: how to keep your body in shape, how to obey strict Catholic directives without ever questioning them, and how to be a fascist.

Hammertoe Mother: when at the beach, Mother would hide her feet in the sand to prevent others from seeing her hammertoes, whereas other mothers hid mostly their heads.

Things you can do with loo-paper: When still at Madrid university, I submitted a short collection of poems to a national poetry competition, and a couple of months later I attended the prize-giving ceremony. The prize was awarded to a well-known writer. I sat in a large hall in some official building, listening as that celebrated writer read a selection from her winning and very tame book. I thought her poems were outdated, dreary, barren, closely aligned with the existing regime, backward, unliterary. Curiously I had just done some shopping (for I was living away from Father's home by then), and in my bag I had several basic products, including a couple of rolls of loo-paper. And I had an idea. What if I get up, walk a few paces to where this established and aging woman is reading and place a roll of loo-paper on the table beside her. I will not have to say a thing because the loo-paper will speak for me and clearly express what I think of her writing and of this corrupt literary competition and of the whole fascist establishment. I considered this possibility throughout the reading and the Q&A and the closing words by the presenter of the event. And all that time my hand was on the loo-roll inside my bag, about as I was to take it out and place it somewhere visible to display my discontent. But I could not bring myself to do it, I simply could not. And just as well, I suppose. Had I done it, would my action have proved that I was stubborn or courageous, a bad loser or a pioneering poet, a gratuitous aggressor or a true fighter? What is certain is that I would have ended up in jail, such were the times. Back then, even loo-paper was not as innocuous as it is today.

Women committing *jigai*, the female version of *seppuku* and which involved cutting the jugular, had their legs tied together to avoid an indecent posture when dying.

Grandfather went back to building *armonios* singlehandedly at the end of his life. Initially he had owned a factory making musical instruments, until he lost his business and began working for the national railway, which I have mentioned already here. One of his later creations was housed in a church in Madrid, the musical backdrop accompanying all those ceremonies that highlight a life. Because of its very rich and dark tone, that particular harmonium was more suited for funerals than for christenings, that is what he was told. I am sure the harmonium is still in use; there may be fewer births nowadays, but death is still going strong.

Guilt has been inflicted upon me, here to stay: what I should have done, and why I did not do things better, and how it was all my fault. Guilt fans the flames of mental well-being, making my mind vulnerable and tenuous. Everything seems to make me feel guilty, even the things I did not do. I take it that all these feelings of guilt stem from my stern Catholic upbringing, whereby children are born already bearing a sin, guilty of someone else's alleged error and disobedience; in other words, first you are accused and then you have to prove your innocence. Guilt was imposed on me from above, but it attacked well below the belt.

In her case, kidney stones normally seem to be about a centimetre in length, derived from calcium oxalate, and make an appearance every seven years to the day as if performing a ritual in her name.

There is a word for the fear of being touched: haphephobia. It used to be a rare condition, but now it is not so uncommon. Because of the pandemic, you could say. Or perhaps because we have all now genuinely decided that we wish to be left alone.

She was always afraid that she had underperformed and was nothing but an understudy, until she unlearnt the old and obsolete lines, and began writing a fresh script that started with the sentence: "And now in my own words."

In the days when education and learning were not so readily available in a ravaged country, correspondence courses were highly regarded and one of the best ways of expanding knowledge. As well as attending high school, I did a couple of two-year correspondence courses on the subjects of Drawing and Guitar, with some of the best tutors there were at the time. After the civil war, many teaching staff had left the country, and those who stayed behind lost their posts or were jailed. Teachers would not be allowed back to teaching in schools or universities until decades later. Thus, correspondence course tutors were among the best. Like most activities that appealed to the intellect and the imagination, education and teaching were considered potentially threats to the regime.

These are the things that irritate her beyond measure: meanness, discourtesy, rowdiness, inanity and, most of all, inequality.

One day I came up with a solution to perfectionism: I started doing things imperfectly, even leaving things half-done. And it was all fine, by any standards.

Just like Mr. Rochester, for years I had a secret mental patient in my life. I have lived with a neurodivergent child for a long time, and she is now an adult. No diagnosis, no assistance, no support, no acknowledgement. It was a carefully guarded secret, and very few outside the family circle or among my closest friends knew that we had this insurmountable problem. We tried everything: costly treatments, endless efforts to appease her, giving in to whatever she demanded, total and unconditional love. I was convinced that providing her with everything she needed or wanted was the solution; it turned out that the more I gave, the weaker and more vulnerable I appeared to be. The situation became unmanageable and out of control, and there were long periods when either she kept away or we kept away, whatever our blood bonds. Despite the commotion and despair, I never gave up on her and I continued trying everything, anything, even at the expense of neglecting other members of the family, myself included. She was eventually diagnosed with a series of neurodivergent conditions and put on medication. I would have wanted her to seek other professional opinions and advice, since the drugs she was on helped just marginally, and perhaps different therapies would have been more effective. She would regularly say: "You do not understand!" and she was right; only a medical expert can comprehend such unrestrained and fear-provoking traits, the hell that her mind would create for herself and for others; thus, it became a matter for professionals to deal with, and not the family. Doing our very best to survive made us stronger, though the feeling did not last forever; sometimes it weakened our resolve and we wanted to give up and go our separate ways; in all, trying to cope with her condition left us depleted and broken in so many ways, with a terrible sense of failure and loss. For her, it was heart-breaking that the family seemed to abandon her at times, but she had to find her own path and forge her own life as she was so very fortunately blessed with intelligence, creativity, talent and resolve in spades. For us, none of the approaches we attempted could bring us peace or closure: being superhumanly courageous, though this was exhausting and could not be sustained for long; adopting an impassive attitude and resorting to accepting fate without complaint;

pretending that it was not happening, so that it would all go away; taking refuge in despondency and anguish; and finally yet futilely asking: "What did I do to deserve this, after all my hard work and sacrifices rearing children and my selfless parenting...?" The answer, both for her and for us, can only be found in a cartoon of 'Hägar the Horrible' by American artist Dik Browne: the first frame says "Why me?" and the second frame says "Why not?"

The final stertor of death: its terrifying sound never to be forgotten; the reluctance of the self to return to nothingness, whence it once came; a singularly dramatic yet most assertive way of Father saying goodbye.

I realised only today that a small multicoloured statue of Buddha with a Scottish beret and made by one of my children when at primary school, was in fact a small multicoloured statue of Buddha, with a Scottish beret, and made by one of my children when at primary school.

If you are not careful, she will include you in one of her books.

Teenage girls at the time had to do something called *servicio social*, the female equivalent of military service. It was administered by the branch of the fascist political party in power that dealt with women's issues and was fittingly called *Sección Femenina*. As an indoctrination tool, the *servicio social* was compulsory if you wanted to get a job or continue into further education, or even apply for a passport. With a duration of six months, it included training on religious and political issues, followed by a few months helping out in schools or hospitals, without any type of remuneration. In my case, I was exonerated from having to do the *servicio social* for the simple reason that I had worked so very hard at being a housewife and looking after my home when Mother died, whilst also being a student. I was elated when I learnt that I did not have to do the *servicio social* –I had received enough fascist indoctrination as it was.

"You must rest!" the doctors demand of me. But what can I do, since I am always at the coalface?

Moths and mice and head lice were not the only parasites that I had to endure at home. He also entered my life and sucked me dry.

There is something called *post-coital tristesse*; it sounds much more thought-provoking than the event it follows.

One of my stories is about a writer who, when writing on the subject of the end of the world, decided to sharpen her pencil without realising that she was actually destroying the world that existed inside the tip of that pencil. I have been asked many times about the meaning of this story. Did I want to say that the sole act of writing about the end of the world brings the world, as we know it, to its end? Or is it that there are many worlds around us, everywhere, even inside the lead of a pencil? Or could the story signify that the history of the world is being written by someone who does not care much about the whole thing, an entirely impassive and detached creator of some sort? Well, the meaning of my story is not for me to say.

In shaking up her demons, she must avoid driving away her angels.

The relationship turned out to be completely unforeseen. It was not what you get in self-help books about couple survival, but something altogether different, a kind of symbiotic arrangement where two individuals are attached to each other in a unique kind of way. They are not lovers, nor friends, nor are they related. It is basically a novel way of sharing a life. So do not judge me by your dreary customs and arrangements, or by centuries-old habits about how to live life. I do it my way, and if I have broken rules or not lived up to other people's expectations, *je m'en fous*.

My old dresses were always sent by post to one of my first cousins. Three years older than me, she was very small for her age, which was most probably due to the lack of proper nourishment during those difficult times in the country. My father would send her widowed mother a monthly allowance, as they were extremely deprived. Their father, my father's younger brother, died because of the post-war scarcity and the hard physical work he had to engage in to make ends meet. After his death, the family basically had to live from the handouts that others provide. Once a year we would visit our widowed aunt and her three children. During one of our yearly visits, my cousin and I were running around their tiny yard chasing their chickens in what was a highly enjoyable game, and I felt in my soul the intense joy that she radiated. I had a sudden realisation, even though I was so young: this sweet and cheerful girl was enjoying life to the full despite all the difficulties she was facing. And I – a prim, smart, clean, polished, cultured little girl– belonged to a very different and self-congratulatory world that needed to do its bit of charity to feel good about itself.

To be able to share your passion for a film or a piece of writing or a work of art, that is true love.

People approach you not to enquire about how you write, not to ask questions regarding the marvel of changing events into words like water into wine, not to show a deep interest in your characters, dialogues or descriptions, not to seek enlightenment or elucidation, but to tell you in no uncertain terms that they also write. The usual account is that they have a book inside them; or in the case of those who have progressed somewhat, they tell you that they are attending a creative writing course and then talk about how the stories they write are no worse than the stories they read. I do not think that too many people have ever given any thought to what it is that drags a writer through life and never once lets go, making you frantic if you are not sacrificing everything on the altar of this insufferably demanding goddess. And even when you do what is required of you, the resulting writing can never be good enough, for there is a second and much more terrifying character in this whole drama: the harshest judge lurking inside the furthermost recesses of your mind and condemning as worthless every single thing that you write.

Those facets of her that she chooses not to display publicly, sometimes show vibrantly in what she wears.

Grandmother always said that she was a descendant of Juan Bravo, who led the Castilian Revolt of the *Comuneros* in 1520, in defiance of regal authority. It appears that, over the centuries, a particular branch of the family with the Bravo surname unusually adopted a 'b' to replace the 'v'. Thus, when asked what her surname was, Grandmother would always specify: "*Brabo, con dos bes.*"

Forgetting things seems to be the norm at this stage in life. If I do not write an idea immediately when it crops up, it is thrown forever into the gloomiest and deepest pit, never to be recovered; I call it my dark sea of oblivion.

After a certain age, falling desperately in love does not mean that you must act on it –love is but a happy thought.

I was told by a photographer I once had a relationship with that the best photographs are those that are never shot. By that same token, the best bits in this book were perhaps, inadvertently or not, discarded by the wayside or left on the cutting-room floor or forgotten in an electronic file called 'Left out'.

Fear of the unknown is the usual human trait. But there is also fear of the known, which is a much shittier thing.

Ah, translation: at work I was invited to a dinner with someone in a position of authority, let us call him Y, and most people there were total sycophants by a mile. Towards the end of the meal, we all got talking about language, and Y said that his favourite word meant Z in English, but not exactly, but almost there, but not quite. He went on to comment on how difficult it was to translate that single word Z with precision, as there were many nuances that you would need to leave behind if you had to choose only one word out of the many equivalent options in the target language. And I breathed deeply, and I replied that if a single word gives you all that trouble, sir, imagine how difficult it is for us translators in this organization to translate a sentence, or a paragraph, or a page, or a whole document, or the thousands and thousands and thousands and thousands of pages we must deal with as professionals year after year. As expected, Y said not a thing and there was a general gasp among the people there which took about a minute to die down. On my part, I was so very happy because I had come across Z, a new and fascinating word.

Someone once mistakenly said that a mystique was born around me, for I was not always visible, attainable, available.

Yes, I had two vaginal births where you had to push like you wanted to raise the Titanic.

In those days even the big C was considered contagious, and so at home we burnt Mother's designer dresses in the furnace and disinfected her gold jewellery with ethanol.

There used to be an elephant in the room, but now we have a whole menagerie.

Are you Asian or what, they ask my young child. She is dark, with jet eyes, her hair the colour of a black hole if I ever saw one. She knows not the word *xenophobia*, but she suspects that there is an ugly idea lurking in the background in search of a willing proponent.

Roughly speaking, words will follow you like loyal soldiers if you valiantly lead them into battle and are selflessly willing to die in their name.

People fuse bizarre combinations; it does not necessarily follow that if you are a good citizen, you are also a nice human being; that if you do not steal from others, you are decent; that if you do not kill, honourable. Yes, you could be squeaky clean and with no sins up your sleeve, but you leave others distraught and depressed because you do not ever ask them about their dreams.

Unavoidably, all these words have become one long meditation without me realising.

Pamela, Tracy, and me. I am not concealing any names here. In the same ward, all affected by strokes, whether ischaemic or haemorrhagic, bleed or clot for the layperson. Pamela, probably in her 80s, is lying on a bed across me and tragically cannot move or do anything for herself. Tracy is much younger; she is in the bed next to mine and replies to the question posed by one of the nurses: "How are you feeling today, Tracy." "Like rubbish!" Tracy says. My age is somewhere between Pamela's and Tracy's, and I am not as badly affected as they are. I am lucky, for I can still move and speak, although I cannot do either properly for now. But the questions remain forever: will this happen again, will it be worse next time, could it be final, will I ever be myself once more.

"This is how we do it in this country!" several mothers said to me many years ago when I arrived to watch a netball match at school and asked why on earth were the children playing in sub-zero temperatures.

Grandmother knew all the old songs by heart and would sing them to me: *'Niña de los ojos negros'*, *'El rosal produce espinas'*, *'Apágame ese lucero'*, *'Escúchame dos palabras'*, *'La Tarara'*, *'De los álamos vengo, madre'*...

I sit down for lunch and observe that every single one of my actions has been consistently developing over millions of years: the first hunger pang... the first morsel... the first time someone decided that cooking was preferable to eating raw food... the first rich sauce... the first *paella*... the first ever yawn after a hearty meal...

At my school in Madrid (single sex, a convent school), the subject of the day is Adam and Eve, and I decide that it is imperative that the class discusses both evolution and apes, along the lines of several books I have read, even a forbidden book about a naked ape that I have somehow managed to get my hands on. Any questions? the nun asks. I can think of several things. We are but hominins. Complex advancements in our genes made us what we are today. If you wait long enough, things happen: life makes an appearance, music is composed, poetry is written, artists produce art. Yes, I try to say all these things in a rushed, almost desperate way. And Adam and Eve? the nun asks. Whilst Adam represented all men, I reply, Eve represented herself and, being as she was a rebel, she used her own mind to make a decision and was regrettably blamed in the process as the instigator of everything that is wrong with the world for all History to behold. Could it not be that the story of Adam and Eve is roughly emblematic, I add, so that things are not called by their name but by something that the vast majority can understand? I speak thus to the whole classroom, moving my arms elaborately. Some girls muffle their laughter, for it could be that this little episode has sparked uncertainty in their minds. Most girls in the classroom are probably swearing to never speak to me again; me, the girl who seems to be from another country in her own country, and whose Spanish is not as perfect as theirs, as if she is still learning it. The nun teaching us is a competent professor of History and Theology. She has been to Rome and met all the right people in high places. She has travelled the world with the sole purpose of converting anything that moves to the true faith. And as I am about to continue, she makes an announcement in the classroom about how next week we shall be discussing the story of Moses crossing the Red Sea. But evolution, I interrupt (oh, the dreaded word), is the explanation. And that is because evolution is not only the verified truth, but it also sounds respectable when said in a loud and melodramatic voice, as I am doing right now. *"¡Evolución!"* But the nun will have none of it and continues to announce the parting of the Red Sea as if it were to happen there and then. Wait and hear all about it! Evolution, I say again during the morning break, but now as a whisper. Like Eve, I seem to be representing only myself.

And one day I decided to do things differently for the simple reason that what I have done until now did not work. I am then asked: "How do you know it did not work?" And I reply: "Well, it has produced nothing but sorrow." And then a final question is put to me: "Is there anything but sorrow?"

Is this a memoir or an *aide-mémoire*, I hear you asking.

What she wants to know about people when she first meets them are their politics and their religion, the two areas of discussion that should traditionally be avoided at all costs. But as she sees it, once both parties agree on these two subjects (or putting it in a different way, any newcomers in her life prove that they think for themselves), then she can go about the business of being friends with them.

Some years after Mother died, Father was diagnosed with bowel cancer and passed away within months. Was it a physical or a mental trigger that caused it, and who was responsible: the war; the wounds acquired in combat; his children, all of whom eventually left the family home; his unfulfilled dreams; the deaths he experienced close-up and possibly the deaths he inflicted on the battlefield; the sadness of not having become an artist as a young man, nor a children's writer when he retired? But there was probably another war in his life: *"En guerra con mis entrañas,"* as Machado wrote.

Unrequited love can also be put to good use. We can dress it up and feel falsely yet sweetly nostalgic about what could have taken place. This sort of love, inexistent and imaginary, can enthuse us to no end –because it never happened, we enrich it as we wish and make it utterly perfect. And even better: it can be usefully recycled for scripted love-scenes, allowing us to revel in the thought that it is for real when reading out our final draft.

It could well be that I have already started to die. In stages. Little by little. Am already dead. Was never truly living. Dying a kind of death. In the same way that there are many ways of being alive, there must be multiple ways of being dead.

Fashion is never a matter of wearing an item, but of possessing it.

My dystopian novel *'El tiempo que falta'*, rejected so many times until it was finally published, began like this:
 –¡*Soy yo... pero no soy yo!*
 Frente al espejo del cuarto de baño, la imagen de un hombre joven de larga cabellera negra y sonrisa insolente pasó a ser, en un abrir y cerrar de ojos, la imagen de un hombre maduro con cuatro madejas de cabellos enredados y expresión de pavor. Lo que pudo haber sucedido entre uno, afeitándose, y otro, también afeitándose, era imposible de traer a la memoria. Peor aún, las dos imágenes se produjeron una detrás de otra, como si entre ambas no hubiera habido nada en absoluto. Si se trataba de una

broma pesada, o un error de cálculo, o un mero ensueño de la mañana, por el momento no había manera de saberlo.

—Es sólo una pesadilla... —dijo para sí, pellizcándose la palma de la mano y profiriendo un grito más de miedo que de dolor.

Sentía un sabor amargo en la boca y se pasó la lengua por los labios, antes tan suaves y ahora tan ásperos. En las sienes sintió varias sacudidas que nunca había sentido antes, y no se le ocurrió más que golpearse la cabeza contra la puerta del baño.

—¿Yo? —preguntó, frotándose la frente arrugada y unas mejillas hundidas sin remisión.

Sí, había envejecido sin más y ya no era el hombre joven y vigoroso de hacía unos instantes. En lugar del semblante mordaz de siempre había ahora una mirada de pánico, hasta su extraordinaria energía había cedido paso a un cansancio devastador. Sólo los ojos tenían la arrogancia de siempre.

—¿Pero qué ha pasado? ¿Qué ha sido? —preguntó a gritos, dándose cuenta de que también su voz había cambiado, y además para peor.

Con una toalla se limpió la espuma de afeitar que aún le quedaba en la barbilla y nuevamente miró de soslayo al extraño del espejo. Se trataba de una persona ajena a su vida, un total desconocido. Lo que él era había desaparecido sin mayor explicación, y algo muy diferente lo había reemplazado. ¿Una tragedia o apenas una farsa?

—La suplantación, perfecta. Pero la sustitución, mediocre...

One day I saw an ad in the paper: English teachers sought for private language school in central Madrid. I applied to the job and was granted an interview. And during the interview, held in English with the director of the place who had a heavy Spanish accent and made countless grammatical errors, I was told: "But you have a Spanish surname, and we cannot have an English teacher with a Spanish surname." I was born in Spain, I replied, but I lived as a child and adolescent in the UK. "Well, he said, we need you to be British. So, we will change your name; you are now Miss Rivers. And to sound convincing you must have a British accent when speaking Spanish." I dithered for a week and then phoned to accept the offer. I was young and I needed both the money and the experience. As requested, I became Miss Rivers and adopted a British accent when speaking Spanish in the classroom. I was extremely uneasy in the role, to say the least, and my frustration got worse as time went by. A couple of times I forgot to put on a British accent when speaking Spanish, and the students looked at me in disbelief. One day I decided that I could not continue conning anyone, least of all my students with many of whom I had developed a friendship. To the director's great surprise, I resigned. I want to come clean, I said, I cannot continue with the charade. A few weeks later I contacted some of my students by phone to tell them the truth: that I had been born in Madrid and brought up in London, that I spoke Spanish without an accent, and that my name was not Miss Rivers. To my surprise, they took it very lightly, some of them even thought it was all a bit of fun, but I was mortified all the way. Deception is no small thing. I myself have been duped several times and, when it happens, I always remember Miss Rivers as if it was payback time.

There came a day when there was no need to prove anything (beliefs, character, attitudes) and I kind of retired in the very real sense of the word from all those things that seemed to move others deeply but did nothing for me any longer.

The catastrophic nature of her being? Of her being what?

Perhaps the circumstance that –whether unwittingly or willingly– he had been working for American intelligence (use any acronym you like) in his afternoon job after he finished his morning shift at the Ministry, explains it all. Spain was excluded from the Marshall Plan, but the US still decided to invest in the country. It was a gigantic scheme that desperately needed locals who spoke English. More importantly, the American government required a stronghold in Europe, even though they had to deal with a transgressor of rights, the last European dictator who reinvented himself as a saviour and miserably left a lasting and calamitous legacy in his image and likeness. Is that why Father was approached by the other side? And why they approached him at a party, for everyone to see? All this needs to be further researched.

They may not love me how I want them to love me, but they still love me.

Grandfather developed a serious liver infection, possibly because of a hydatid cyst or cystic echinococcosis. This type of cyst is transmitted from animals to humans; in other words, hydatid disease is a type of zoonotic disease, now very much in the headlines because of Covid. At the time it was believed that Grandfather had been infected by our lovely pet dog, as both our dog and cat were kept at our grandparent's house whilst we were in London and even after we returned to Madrid. But there was another theory about Grandfather's illness: he only ever ate eggs, usually for lunch and sometimes for supper as well, which was not a proper diet by any standards. Heartbreakingly, Grandfather never recovered from his illness and died shortly after his seventieth birthday. He was an extraordinary human being; had answers to all your questions; was massively knowledgeable on many subjects; owned specialised books of every kind, from Medicine to Art and from technical manuals to History books; could repair any home gadget or small appliance; made toys for us out of wood; knew how to build musical instruments as I discuss elsewhere in this memoir. He had a solution to every problem, except unsurprisingly to the very last problem of all.

Today, I declare that my favourite ballet is 'La Bayadere'; my favourite opera is 'Lucia de Lammermoor'; my favourite film is 'Hiroshima, mon amour'; my favourite author is Gogol; my favourite artist is Holbein. But tomorrow, who knows.

In wanting to cry, I laughed in the face of misfortune. It is the healthier and more sensible option of the two.

At this age, she plays no roles beyond what she is, suffers no fools, takes no shit.

When you are burying your mother, not you personally but someone doing it in your name; not burying with a shovel or a pick to break up the soil, but above ground, in one of those burial niches; not exactly your mother, because what is a dead body except for fragments of flesh and bone held together one last time before the unstoppable process of decay. So, as I was saying, when you are burying your mother, in a figurative way, it is best to walk, without too much fuss, right behind the coffin along the predetermined paths of a Madrid cemetery, *Cementerio del Oeste* as it was known then, though the burial grounds will soon make way for colossally overpriced apartments, the living taking over the land of the dead, and whyever not since death is not just for the privileged few. And as I was saying, when you are burying your mother you have to follow the funeral cortège as close as you possibly can without, naturally, encumbering those carrying the coffin, and whom you do not recognise, for they are not members of your family nor friends but total nobodies, possibly professional mourners paid by the undertaker to flex their muscles, or perhaps they are doing it out of love for an unknown woman, that would certainly be a generous gesture, her ex-fiancés, boys she once kissed, men who admired her secretly, all those she would have wanted to sleep with but stopped in her tracks because the country was mired in the most regressive and soul-numbing traditions. But I must not get carried away with thoughts of love at a time of death. You therefore try to walk as close as possible to the funereal grouping so that, if all those roses so cleverly placed above the coffin were to fall to the ground, you could surely pick them up and keep them forever as a memento of such a terribly sad day. And as it happened, with the heaving and the swaying of a coffin carried by men you have never seen before, and will probably never see again, as I said earlier, one, but one, single red rose falls almost on your hand, and when you reach out it drops to the ground, and as you slow down to collect it, the coffin has moved on, placed as it is on those unfamiliar shoulders, as I said before, and you have to quicken your pace and get on with it, but now with a red rose in your hand, which makes the whole experience a little more interesting and little less desolate and you turn your thoughts to getting hold of another rose. If only you could manage a second rose, that would be even better, or three or four, a bouquet in fact made up of roses meant for the dead. But it is proving to be difficult to reach the top of the coffin where the roses are placed, and the procession is moving so fast, too fast in fact because this is a solemn occasion and things should be slowed down as much as possible. For what is death but the total slowing down of everything you know, no need to rush anywhere ever again and no urges to do anything anymore, no further running around or hurrying up. And when you finally get to where the burial niche is located, the whole spectacle comes to a halt, with everyone who surrounds you a total unknown, as I said before, and you cannot see friends or family when you need them most. In such a setting, there is only one question you can ask: is this it, is this the end of the road for everyone here, because, for all we know, we may also have got caught up in the expiration of things, and this sort of ending might well be catching and we are all going to die and disappear right now, this is what your agile and young mind thinks; and before you can blink in that cemetery in the western part of the city, the coffin is already being raised by what looks like a makeshift crane and then placed inside an empty socket, for there is no place for the dead underground anymore. The dead have to be housed up in the air, in constructions of empty sockets that are then closed with a plaque stating name, memorable years and some kind of phrase to give some kind of sense to the whole thing, if it has any. And all this time, there is this rose in your hand and you cannot stop thinking that you must never let go of it, for it is the only thing you have from that momentous day. You promise yourself that you will preserve the rose forever, housed in a special case made of glass, and you will look at it every day and will remember what Mother was, her life, her illness, her death, the day of her burial, your own running after the coffin, the red rose that fell almost onto your hands. And with those thoughts in mind, you manage a smile, though you know deep down that the rose will not last forever, and its petals will come apart and dry and fall into oblivion. And what happens is that you somehow misplace the rose when you get home, and it disappears from your possessions, never to be found again. And you will forget that day for most of your life because running after a coffin to get hold of one of the roses deposited kindly on top of its lid makes no sense whatsoever in the wider expanse of things.

I hear you asking about what I omitted from this memoir. As expected, I left out all those memories that by now I have totally forgotten. I wonder what has become of them with no one to cherish them lovingly.

"We must acknowledge her book, for she is a born writer, *es una escritora nata*. But we cannot give her the award because what she has written is nothing but a collection of short stories and not a novel. Prizes should be given exclusively to novels, because the novel is the preferred Art form above all others. Whereas the short story is the lesser exercise. Thus, if she is not a novelist, she is a lesser writer."

As an officer, even though retired by then, Father kept a revolver at home. In his final months, he could be seen mostly in the sitting room, with the revolver in his hand. He appeared to be not so much holding the weapon as caressing it. His emaciated face and gauntness were by now disturbing. Yes, the revolver would avoid the pain of the grand finale and shorten the journey, plus you could get to conveniently choose the day and the time, instead of all the waiting and the uncertainty. Which is another way of saying that one could be a commanding master and not a willing servant. In his right hand, the revolver; in his left hand, a very large glass of the best cognac. Under the influence of alcohol, he was trying to decide whether to wait for the end imposed or to trigger the end chosen. Eventually it became clear that to stick around and see how it would all unravel was a matter of honour. Death would happen anyway, soon enough, with or without a gun, with or without an alcoholic prop.

And one of my favourite pastimes was ironing silver chocolate wrappings with my fingers and keeping them inside the pages of books as my most prized possession.

Foreplay was consensual, but not the final lap. Final lap? Do you hear what you are saying? It might have been the final lap for him, but was it for you? Do you, as a woman, have a final lap, or is it just one more lap, before the next one, and the next one, and the next, and the very next?

When I returned to London in my early twenties, I had to live in a damp and creepy basement for a while. It was a small flat with a bathroom, but no lavatory. I shared a communal lavatory with the shop on the ground floor, which was no fun. Plus, the flat had a constant smell of gas and grime, and I would spend my days bleaching the whole place. I was so unhappy that I would go for long walks in the only open space nearby, Brompton Cemetery. I became obsessed with the idea that the dead were so much closer to the surface of the earth than I was. Who is more alive, I would ask, when walking around those two hundred thousand graves? Perhaps like Balzac I should have taken the names and the stories from all the tombs that I came across during my walks.

So that she does not feel trapped in only one role, she plays many roles, as best she can, and some she enjoys and some she does not. A few of the roles she plays she likes, and they are still going strong. Regarding the roles she has never played but would love to, she is sure that she would be very good at playing them but she has not yet been given the chance. Finally, there are roles that she neither likes nor dislikes, and performs them routinely without eagerness or passion, aware that she could easily live without them, and yet she does nothing to change the course of things because this may weirdly be the only way to fulfil her true destiny.

Although Mother was concerned about what people would think if they knew her daughter had consulted a psychiatrist –and that is why she forbade it– one day she came home with several books by Freud translated into Spanish. I devoured them all, even if I did not understand them fully, neither the language nor the ideas. It might have been her way of making up to me.

After a certain age, the very tragic stories of your past, and which caused you so much grief in their day, have now been reduced to plain after-dinner anecdotes.

We were led to believe that Father was pretty inept as most things and that Mother ran the show. To this day, I have analysed this unfortunate situation and have not yet been able to understand why such a state of affairs was allowed to persist. Father was the one with the imagination and the flair and the fun. His sense of humour was dry, elegant, overpowering. Mother's humour was basically modest; she was highly intelligent but not ingenious, amazingly alert in any circumstance and with other people but never realising that perhaps her children were a tad unhappy. And yet, we hated Father doing certain things and trusted only Mother. I am referring to basic stuff like driving, for example. Mother would be the one to drive long distances, and when once in the middle of France she was too tired to continue at the wheel, she stopped the car on the kerb and swapped places with Father. And as he was about to drive off, the children opened the passenger doors and stepped out of the car, clearly stating that we would not get back inside unless it was Mother who was doing the driving. I have always wondered about the cruel effect this kind of event had on Father and, more importantly, how it shaped a child's vision of the world.

I received medals both for Scottish dancing and for being in the same job for over twenty years. Let me put it plainly: the former I loved doing; as to the latter, no comment.

I suffer from migraines with auras like zigzags or kaleidoscopes, as if I had my very own TV test card. I also suffer from vestibular neuronitis, which annoyingly makes you horribly dizzy without getting high; it is a problem relating to the labyrinth in your inner ear and it attacks you with uncontrollable vertigo. I have an auto-immune ailment, which affects the nether regions and the name of which escapes me at present. I sometimes have stretches of insomnia that, although not an illness, does leave you disheartened for the rest of the day; the cause is probably having far too many uncalled-for things on my mind. And there is always the threat of ischaemic episodes; such episodes are very much a last resort of the body telling you that something is wrong and that you might well be approaching the very end if you do not take adequate measures such as, for example, *lie low* and *be present* and *move slowly and gently* and *harken only to words that are essential...*

Imperfection, impermanence, incompleteness should be used in everyday speech without fear of reprisal.

Simply put, I arrived by plane just in time for the agony. Once in the hospital room, I could not stop sobbing: *"¡Perdóname, perdóname, perdóname!"* Some of us had done him untold damage, and I ardently asked to be forgiven. But it was all happening so quickly that Father had no time to exonerate me; he was far too busy dying to pay any attention to my wailing and left this world without ever knowing how remorseful I was. An apology that has not been accepted, even if only because of lack of time, you will forever carry on your shoulders.

He was well-known for trying it with most women in the workplace. S for stalker; or if you prefer, S the stalker. With some women it was just touching and feeling here and there, and with others he would go all the way, in any location, at any time. Yes, promises of abandoning his wife and family were made on a daily basis. I was lucky in a way, because nothing major happened when he assaulted me inside a lift and tried to touch whatever he could get his hands on. What I naively said to him as the lift doors closed was: *"¿Qué estas haciendo? ¡Estoy casada y tengo hijos!"* And what S the stalker cynically replied was: *"¡Yo también!"*

And so, this is silence:

Scars are a sign that you have been to some kind of war, whether on the battlefront or the homefront, and managed somehow to survive, sometimes barely. In my case, the first scar was the strawberry on my head, as I have mentioned. Not a real strawberry but a cyst of an unidentifiable kind, in pink hues and surrounded by pimples that looked like the tiny grains on the skin of berries. The family always spoke about the strawberry that I had as a baby and not about the cyst, so that the sensitive child would not end up downcast, because she sometimes displayed signs of too vivid an imagination. The new narrative would help and encourage me, they thought: the going was that if I could grow strawberries on my head, then I could probably do anything in my life. So, this is the story of my strawberry. And if we stay on the subject of scars and injuries, there's a scar on my left eyelid, the result of removing a sebaceous cyst when I was an adolescent; I conceal it by painting the eyelid in silver and blue to match my favourite dress. And then we get very personal: a scar runs from my waist diagonally all the way downwards, the one kept under wraps for no one to see; this is a really terrible scar, not smooth and rectilinear but clunky and messy, the result of an appendectomy, with peritonitis, gangrene and imminent death as backdrop; doctors managed to save me in the end, but I have this scar to remember all of them by, and I have discussed this medical episode in these pages. I have even more private scars as a result of two vaginal births: the first episiotomy performed with the precision of a scalpel and it all turned out well; the second, I triggered myself because I pushed when I should not have pushed, and the tearing of flesh ran from the vaginal opening to the perineum in a crisscrossed, cracked, ugly sort of way. And then, there are small scars stemming from procedures performed with microsurgery: two small scars on my back to remove kidney stones; and finally, the very visible scars on my left shoulder because of a torn rotator-cuff and subsequent infection, which was most probably the result of carelessness or negligence during the operation, so much so that the surgeon refused to include my case in his medical portfolio. Such are the physical scars of a life; then there are all the others.

Seemingly the dead can do nothing for her, yet they will speak up if she happens to ask them an important question.

Hope springs eternal in the hearts of both those with a passionate desire and those who uphold emptiness as a way of life.

Father always said he had forgotten about the war, but I knew this not to be true. It was a wish more than anything, because the war had very seriously damaged him; his reluctance to be emotional or demonstrative can undoubtedly be attributed to his oppressed childhood, but more so to his harrowing experiences on the battlefront. When further asked by outsiders, requesting even a single memory of the war, he would say that he did not want to talk about it. But from time to time, he would give us, his children, a few scraps of information, and this is how we learnt about some of the episodes in which he had been involved during the conflict. The saving of the position on a hill, which I have mentioned, was the main one. We also asked him about killings during the war, and we wanted to know whether he had inflicted pain and suffering. He said that he had only ever killed when he was coming out of the trenches or when he was waiting for the enemy to come out of the trenches and thus stop them from attacking. *"En defensa propia"* he added. *"¿Sólo en defensa propia?"* we asked, perhaps disbelieving him. And we asked about executions, lowering our eyes. And Father said that he had never executed anyone, as in a firing squad, and that he had allowed prisoners to escape and was proud of that. Once an enemy soldier, whom Father had released, told him that his descendants and Father's descendants would meet one day and make peace. This story made us cry. And then we asked about his worst memory. And he too lowered his eyes and told us that his worst memory was when the enemy threw a grenade that tore away part of his upper arm and back. And yet the enemy soldiers did not leave Father to die but carried him on a stretcher all the way to one of their war hospitals –

as a prisoner, of course– and the doctors there saved his life. When sometime later Father recovered, he managed to escape; crossing enemy lines, he went all the way back to his battalion. He recalled the cold, the misery, the stench of death; travelling by foot along huge stretches of land, trying to avoid getting caught; crossing towns and villages, concealing who he was and what side he fought for. Finally, after some weeks, he re-joined his own forces, and had to convince them that what he had gone through was nothing but true. But they would always be suspicious of Father: how come enemy soldiers had saved him instead of executing him, how come they had treated his wounds, how come he had escaped so easily and crossed enemy lines and managed to return. Perhaps Father was an informer, perhaps a Republican sympathiser, perhaps a traitor. This cloud of uncertainty would always hang over Father. Hence what happened decades later.

Someone in my family, I cannot remember who it was, would always say this about love: "*En todas las relaciones sentimentales, uno quiere y el otro se deja querer.*"

Destiny has generously taken me to many exquisite places: from Vancouver to the Black Sea – from the Pitti to the Cisterna Basilica – from the Duoro to the Rhône – from Central Park to Skye – from Ait Ben Haddou to Monet's lily pond in Giverny – from Ludwig's Neuschwanstein Castle to the Mosque-Cathedral of Córdoba – from Mont-Saint-Michel to Brooklyn Bridge – from Knossos to Pompeii – from the Castle of Rivoli to Mariensäule – from a Newyorker Guggenheim to a Basque Guggenheim – from Milan to Sorrento – from the Alps to the Pyrenees – from Puerta del Sol to Salamanca – from Billings to Montauk – from Teide to Vesuvius – from Porto's Sé to Basilica di Santa Maria del Fiore – from Sahara to Tabernas – from Marrakesh to Casablanca – from the Tunisian Coliseum to the Roman Coliseum – from Zürich to Zaragoza – from MOMA to Mumok – from the Eastern Mediterranean in Heraklion to the Western Mediterranean in Castellón – from Whistler to Obergurgl – from Salem to Siena – from Iona Abbey to Lazareto de Mahón – from the Grand Place to Las Ramblas...

Ah, the days when looking for a word meant flicking through a dictionary to distraction: a substantial exertion both physical and intellectual, yet always an enthusing adventure in search for hidden treasures.

Once a month, someone would ring the bell at home and hand us a wooden box, the size of a small suitcase. A simple enough container for something considered truly priceless by some: the box contained a statuette of the Virgin Mary, or rather a version of her under the name *María Auxiliadora*. The box had two little panels that would open to a glass front, and behind this was the statuette. We would get to keep it in the house for a couple of days, before taking it in its box to the next person on an attached list; normally this next person would live in a nearby location, or at least not too far from us. The whole operation was carefully planned and executed, and about once a month the statuette would arrive at our place. It was us, the children, who were in charge of taking it to the next person on the list, and I can tell you that we did not fight about it. The idea was that, during the time we kept it at home, we would light candles to it and pray with much devotion, hoping our requests would soon come true. As well as praying to the image, we decorated it further with dry flowers or ribbons or items of fake jewellery. And, as expected, we inserted a few coins, or even notes into the locked drawer under the box (the key to which we did not have, and I always assumed that the local parish priest had it). I used to think that it was a very pretty statuette, not unlike the dolls I played with back then, and I certainly enjoyed decorating it. I must add that none of the miracles I prayed for ever came true. Or perhaps they did, and I did not realise at the time; or perhaps what ensued was something so much better than what I had asked for. It was all part of the divine plan, as Father would say at most times. A plan just too complex for a simple human mind to understand. And despite the complexity we, as children, were always trying to unravel the mystery and find an explanation. Because there must be an explanation for everything, must there not be, Father, there must be, there must be, there definitely must be an explanation.

You will say goodbye before delving too much because, for lack of time, you cannot get to know anyone with any intensity or get to love anyone deeply enough or get to enjoy anything to the full. Can you now?

I would dream that we met once a year, in a far-away hotel, for old time's sake. Such had been our agreement. When he said that we could only be together in another life, I assumed that what he meant was that we could at least meet up in my dreamworld. After all, a dream is not the life we are living, in the same way that the life we are living is no dream.

If you go to battle, you will perish; if you do not go to battle, you will unquestionably perish.

An unfair game I was asked to play: there are no rules; it can finish at any time without warning; and, worst of all, there are no winners, no prize, no resolution. However, now and again I may be handed a small reward for bearing up: seas flowing or flowers opening or the Moon shining.

The country is no longer what it was, certainly not what it could have been. There is an element of wanting to go back to the past, a deep nostalgia about what was once good and great in their mind. All of this results in a constant confrontation between the old and the new –or to put it more accurately, between the enlightened and the retrograde. Yes, a few still aspire to preserve ancient customs that serve solely to prolong the concept of privilege, and to sustain a way of life that demands you never depart from the norm, however regressive or unfounded or unjust it may be.

And what if I had got it all wrong?

I decided to start my life afresh, and it is too bad if you do not accept my decision.

The subject of sex ceases to be at the forefront on your life as it used to be, and it is now but a faded memory of some long-lost Eden that never really materialised.

Remember that there is no need to draft an exit plan because it has already been drafted in your name.

Anything minimally social exasperates her to the point of disintegration and makes her dread the next minute. She is talking about things like small talk, gossip, chitchat, chatter, discussions on the innate vices of supermarkets and on the perverse delivery options and on the inconveniences of not being able to go on holiday when you feel like it, forgetting that there are so very many who have never gone once on holiday nor tasted the flavour of a short break nor had any kind of respite whatsoever in their difficult lives.

The moment you tell a publisher that you write in two languages, they think and sometimes say that you probably cannot write in either.

Or could it be that I am inside the wrong person, the wrong gender, the wrong age, the wrong nationality, the wrong temperament, the wrong period of history. The story of a life should be a chronicle of all possibilities.

One of my earlier beliefs was that, after a certain age, I would have a good idea of what everything was about. Having reached that age, things seem to me to be even more bewildering. Perhaps I have not waited long enough, and I would need to wait a little bit more, and then after a certain age I will have some kind of idea of what everything is about, but when reaching that age, things might seem even more bewildering, and so after a certain age...

Father is submitted to an interrogation identical to a court martial in everything but name. It is a long dark room, with two armed guards at the door. There are ten officers sitting at the lengthiest mahogany desk (could it double up as a banqueting table?). He is not sitting himself but standing and facing all those men. There is a deathly silence in the room. They want to break him from every flank, as would be expected from soldiers. They pretend to be looking at piles of reports, constantly whispering to each other. Close to an hour he is kept standing in front of them. It is so dark that he cannot see the men's faces nor the looks of the many portraits surrounding them, those oil paintings of officers in uniform who fought for their country and an abject ideology, adhered to the rebel uprising and staged a coup and conquered, all of them on the winning side as if the other side had not fought valiantly for the country and the people. And before those flesh and blood officers say anything, one of them gets up and shows Father several photographs. *"Son fotografías de la fiesta,"* the officer says, explaining that the photographs are from the last party Father attended before he returned to Madrid from London, the party where he spoke to someone he should not have spoken to. Father looks at the photographs. Yes, there he is in the blurry images of photographs taken with hidden cameras at one of many Embassy parties. There were so many parties at the time. Champagne, small talk, women in rich gear, most men in uniform. For some, those were the days; for others, those days have been happily erased. Yes, in the photographs he is indeed talking to various attendees. But then in one of them he is clearly seen talking to one person in particular, uniformed and very stiff. Father is told that it is an officer from the Eastern Bloc, a Soviet officer, and they ask him why the Soviets spoke to him at the party. Father has to muffle a smile, for his mind always sees everything in terms of both tragedy and comedy: this is beyond ridiculous, a kind of court martial held because of a couple of polite exchanges. He replies that it was only small talk, shaking his head as if the subject had no relevance whatsoever. Yes, small talk about London, the swinging sixties, pop music, Nureyev and Fonteyn, the consequences of Kennedy's assassination. And Father ponders; there is plenty of time to ponder because no one is saying anything about the list he has just provided them, with all the officers looking down at their hands resting on the table. An officer hides his smile with a clenched fist, and a more senior one coughs badly as if he should throw up any time. Father cannot for a second believe that the spectacle is for real. He is a loyal and senior officer and fought the war on their side with medals to prove it. He was awarded none other than the Medal for Suffering in the Name of the Motherland. Nothing but. Yes, he admits only to himself that during the war he was never convinced, deep down in his heart, that he was fighting on the right side; if he fought alongside them it was because he happened to live in that part of the country and not the other, the right side of the tracks you could say. And to prove his loyalty he fled from the enemy after his life was saved by them, and perhaps this is why they doubt him. And in any case, he reminds himself that he should have dedicated his life to Art and not war, though that is another story, a much gloomier one. But who is he but a minor player in a country run by the only European dictator who was never duly defeated, merely recycled. Yes, he says to himself, all this has to be a prank, the cheapest nightmare. It is but a kangaroo court delivering a mock court-martial, he stops himself from saying. Or is it? The Soviet Attaché, they repeat several times. Father barely remembers him. An athletic man, Slavic bone structure, with all features drawn in perfect squares, a full head of reddish hair. Or was that the American Attaché? Or even himself, as a young man? Not one of the ten officers in front of him blinks but stares instead as if to avoid thinking or musing. At almost the same time, and with more or less the same words, they all say they have to teach him a lesson so that no other officer, ever, ever, ever will embark on even small talk, any kind of talk for that matter, with any Soviet citizen, least of all an officer and an attaché. They then say that Father must not only be a loyal officer, but that he must show to be a loyal officer. And they add that they will exile him as a punishment. *"¿Exilio?"* Father asks, still not believing them, and even ventures a smile with his question. *"¡Sí!"* comes the answer. *"¿Dónde?"* They do not specify where and they ask him if he has any other questions? No, this is not a dream, and he pinches his hand. But not only his hand hurts now. Yes, there is one question. He asks whether his medals are the reason why he is not being incarcerated. There comes no reply, and the officers again look down at the mahogany table covered with endless files, most of them still unopened. Not many of those sitting there can have the medals he has, Father thinks and almost declares it. And then he is dismissed from the long dark room. He does not say goodbye, or even salute. And the worst thing is that he has not been told where they are going to exile him. Will it be far away from everything he loves, his wife and children? He leaves without knowing what is to become of him. What happens after that is a blur, an unreliable memory. A long and impenetrable and freezing mist. No, he does not believe a thing until he looks around and realises that he is now standing in the main square of the town to which he has been exiled. It is the coldest city in the whole country, you could call it a physical and spiritual Siberia. You could also say that, of all the towns in all the provinces in all the country, this is the one where he will learn about the USSR, at least in climate terms. A city that the Romans made theirs, architecturally speaking. A place to visit and admire perhaps, but not to be exiled to. So similar in fact to the Russian steppe that the snow scenes with Dr Zhivago and Lara were filmed in its outskirts. Where even in deep summer it is dead cold. And at this present moment, the weather is freezing beyond human tolerance. It is January, the wrong time of the year to punish anyone with anything, let alone with exile. And the cold shows in the icy faces of the locals scrutinising him, the exiled officer, as he arrives at his new year-long destination. Perhaps they are all exiles, he thinks looking at their dead cold eyes. Will my eyes be stony cold as well in no time at all? As if a cold war deserved an even colder exile.

Confronted with death, no idea, no dream, no hope, no excitement can make any sense.

He repeats over and over again that he needs to do it. And I reply: Conquer me, discover me, tempt me, seduce me. I am a far-away land, unexplored and unspoilt. I am Earth, not to be reduced to ashes; I am Woman, not to be trifled with. It is about reaching further heights, another realm, another dream, another sentience. But do not say *I need it*. Convince me, do not command me. Entice me, do not propel me. Make me wander, not be trapped.

My child comes back every night pretending nothing has happened, but she is overwhelmingly distressed by the court case she has to attend every morning for two weeks. It is called jury service, but I would call it a sentence imposed on her that will take years to clear. She is probably one of the youngest ever attending jury service. I only learnt about the case when it was over, for she could not discuss the details with anyone for the duration of the trial. It was about rape, violence, crime, and ultimately deception.

My sense of humour, if I have one, is probably made up of three different traditions which I inherited from either circumstances or blood: black humour, or rather a combination of melancholia and absurdity, that stems from the day when I was accused of burying Mother (metaphorically speaking, but I took the comment at face value at the time, and it stuck; I mentioned the incident earlier in this memoir; this also links with what Christopher Hitchens said about it not being possible to have a sense of tragedy without also having a sense of humour). Surreal humour as displayed by Father also influenced me immensely, and among the many humorous stories he would tell us I remember the one about a man who throughout the day would repeat the word *campana* out of the blue, and we all thought that particular story was hilarious. And finally, the childlike humour of Grandmother, who had a wonderfully innocent sense of fun and such contagious laughter; even when, at the end of her life she had to have a colostomy bag fitted, she kept telling us such funny stories to make us smile.

Discurrir was Grandfather's favourite verb. This is what I do –not *pensar*, but *discurrir*. No wonder I am exhausted.

My radio script was rejected because the producer –a single, middle-aged woman living with her very elderly mother– could not understand how I could fit everything in: the scriptwriting, the literary writing, the translating, the husband, the children, the home, the research, the study, the creativity, life in general and dreams in particular. Therefore, the script could be no good.

A tale of two lives: she proposed, he declined; she stayed, he left; she kept to herself, he travelled; she lived, he died; they were always so incompatible.

I spent years of my life in an office, an excruciatingly long time it was. I was living with total strangers for more hours a day than with my family. It was an enclosed environment in every sense, private and secluded, where windows would not open because fresh air might give staff strange ideas. I was exposed to the best and the worst, happiness and grief, colour and dullness. I have always wondered whether I would have learnt so much about both the strengths and failings of human nature had I travelled across the seas as was my original intention.

A WOMAN ALONE

"¡Soy la única persona que te dirá la verdad!" Mother would say. Since her death, I have been desperately trying to find someone who can also tell me the truth.

Things that could have happened but did not: I was dead close to winning a major literary prize; a well-known American author briefly showed huge interest in my work; I could have been the official translator of a renowned poet, but because she was over 90 at the time she never got back to me, and I fear that by now she may be dead; had I used one language as a writer instead of two, I might have greatly bourgeoned; had I focussed on writing alone and not on living; had I been wiser and wilier; had I been greater and exceedingly good; had I not encountered certain episodes that made me into this dejected creature; had I stayed in one country and not moved to another; had my life been different; had I been someone else...

Even as a child I was given chamomile tea for breakfast to keep stress at bay.

When Father retired from being an army officer, he founded a small independent publishing house called *Amigos de Alicia*, after his love for Carroll's works. He published a few children's books, as well as his translations and some of his creations. Shortly afterwards he sadly passed away, and his small publishing house ceased to operate. In his memory, several decades later I founded another small independent publishing house with the same imprint, but this time in English. The name Alice has always been significant because I loved Carroll's books since a young age. In fact, when asked what I would like to call my new baby-sister, I chose the name Alice. It was not to be her first name, but she has always been blessed with a marvellous sense of wonder.

This filled me with enormous courage: in an interview, *prima ballerina* Tamara Rojo said that scary decisions are the ones that have always paid off.

'April in Portugal': the version played and sung by Satchmo touches your core and makes love to every organ you have. But have you heard the version by the famous organist Ken Griffin? Just for this, you will want to defy death so that you can listen forever.

When suspecting any sort of obsessive or compulsive behaviour on the part of the writer, the reader will want to barge in and try to sort things out in the writer's name.

I would go as far as saying that Schubert's Impromptu in B-Flat Major, Op. posth. 142, No. 3, has all the essentials for a perfect life.

La ciudad que me vio nacer no me verá morir; las calles que recorrí mil veces no volveré a pisar; los amigos que juran que me conocen, de mí sólo saben mi nombre; los amantes que morirán con una idea desafortunada de lo que fui; yo misma, convencida de que al final todo me será revelado.

Shortly after our nanny left, all these jewels disappeared from home. I had stupidly shown her the place where I kept my prized possessions. I even explained that these were Mother's rings and necklaces and bracelets, and this was Great-grandmother's *peineta*, a hair-comb made of real tortoiseshell which she would wear when dressing up for major celebrations. The theft of Mother's bracelet, a gold chain of large yet delicate links, was the most painful: Mother wore it until the day before she died, when she removed it from her wrist and placed it inside the cabinet beside her hospital bed as if she somehow knew.

Finding myself praying yet not believing in the holy fairy tale.

I used to be so very romantic, and now I am so very aromantic.

"¿Y tú por qué no eres tan cachonda como ésta?" This is what my boss at the time asked me in the corridor, pointing at my colleague who, that very hot summer, was wearing a strapless dress. He was obviously insulting both her and me. I remember replying in front of other co-workers "*¡Porque soy una persona muy seria!*" (perhaps too severe and youthful and direct a reply), and then running back to my office and banging the door. My temporary contracts dwindled to nothing after this episode, and my boss horribly snubbed my professional standing in public. He is dead now, and so he cannot defend himself from my accusations. In any case, he was always utterly reprehensible, dead or alive.

If the characters are real, they do not necessarily have to sound believable on the page.

Confusion: the intangible present is something that all moments have in common; the intangible present is something that no two moments share.

Is she some kind of germophobe?

"¡Y ahora queremos una novela!" they said. And I replied that I did not have a novel, but that I wrote short stories, like that book of short stories of mine that they had just published. *"¡Inténtalo!"* they said. And I tried, real hard. And after much trying, they flatly rejected my creation, that on-demand novel. And they repeated that they wanted a novel and that they did not believe in short stories, and they added that nobody did. And that if I insisted on writing short stories, I needed to go to another publisher. So, this was the end of my relationship with that publisher; but unexpectedly it was also the beginning of something so much more exhilarating.

When she was tame and submissive, they all seemed to like her. But will they like her now that she has been remodelled into someone else: untamed, almost feral; bold, almost fearless; steadfast, almost unyielding.

Juan de Mena: *"Muerte que a todos convidas, ¿dime qué son tus manjares?"*

For many years I kept my appendix in a jar with formaldehyde. After my appendectomy, it was given to me by the surgeon as some kind of trophy. Occasionally I would show it to those who expressed an interest in the story of my near-death experience, though I confess that not many inquired about this particular episode of my life. Initially the salvaged appendix appeared to be just like the real thing, floating in liquid, with a small piece of intestine attached and various adhesions; in due course though, it looked totally repulsive, like some decomposing stew. I cannot recall what became of it, that small part of me which was removed to save my life. I suppose it was disposed of by someone in the family, probably flushed down the loo because it was nothing more than yet another sample of organic matter, just like everything we have and everything we are.

If luck is on her side, one day she will be a memory too.

Eve should have admitted that there was no way she could have everything in life and that something had to go. Perhaps the apple, perhaps the tree. Even her mate could go; in any case, she could always try and find someone else (surely there must have been others in that vast territory of a place, probably with a more interesting personality than the man she had been assigned to). But what she should never have let go of is Paradise. It is for keeps and must be preserved at all costs; do not let anyone take it away from you. Paradise is the one thing you need to hold on to, even if you have to give up the very fruits of your endeavours.

Because I always asked far too many questions, I could never get enough information. Hence this double life: the real, with so very few of my questions answered; and the unreal, with the answers that I was forced to supply in lieu.

If you have never had the relevant tests done, how do you know for sure whether you are within the dominant societal standards for neurocognitive functioning or, instead, you are basically neurodivergent?

How tired and exhausted you are at work and at home, how many things you do. It is an almost impossible life to be both a working mother and raise a family (though mothers have always worked, and extremely hard, since the beginning of time, what else?). People cannot believe you do so much stuff; and if you tell them, they think that you are lying and that you cannot possibly be capable of all those things or be good at anything. Consequently, it is best to hide the details from everyone; do not say much; stay very still; keep to yourself; avoid giving any kind of explanation when asked; stay silent; smile.

"If I were true to my people, I would kill!" he said. And that is when I decided to leave him.

The word you have been looking for all this time with profound discontent is contentment.

Ah, the medical profession and their promise to cure your many ailments. They diagnosed my appendicitis wrongly and it turned into gangrene (the specialist who first saw me, a Dr N, stated that it was a clear case of gastritis, with a strong recommendation that I place a hot blanket on my abdomen!). A similar misdiagnosis happened with my long-standing backache, which was in reality a kidney stone. Or my thyroid problem, which is not Hashimoto's though it might be, but not really, but who knows, as the endocrinologist said. A horribly torn tendon on my shoulder was not just a sprain but required complicated surgery, followed by an infection, and treated with serious doses of antibiotics and months of rehabilitation. The same with my breaking waters, and they sent me home to a week of agony before giving birth. And what about the suspected transient ischaemic attack that in fact turned out to be two fully blown strokes and various other ischaemic episodes? And the dark patch that appears in the line of vision of my left eye when I get up in the middle of the night? This dark patch is still very much a mystery after several years of medical investigations, an inordinate number of tests, and various consultants later with not a single one establishing what the problem is. But I must be more lenient, and perhaps it is not for doctors to diagnose this particular ailment because it might be something more fictional than real: a phantom of the past interfering with my vision, the blemishes of my present days, a hazy vision of the future, a second existence alongside this one, the mind fading away, the world coming to an end, a melodrama in the making.

Atwood talks about the duplicity of the writer, but I would call it duality.

A story as told by Father: A man had never seen a bison and, when he finally saw one, he exclaimed: "That animal does not exist!"

I already have a natural disposition to social distancing, and therefore the present confinement is no big deal for me from this point of view, but only from this point of view.

Here is the ending of a story of mine about finding your way in a labyrinth, first in English and then in Spanish, both so different in content and form, emotions taking over language: "...stories are as comforting as memories, they say. It is not for us to know that sort of thing, but we can provide motivations for stories, and here are a few: imprisonment, betrayal, deception, unrequited feelings, loneliness. And if you want a few adjectives: insane, ludicrous, incongruous, pointless, stupid. And here are some verbs: to be lost, to feel disoriented, to be confused, to feel abandoned, to be forsaken. And if you were to make up stories about your experiences in the labyrinth, it would be good to memorize all those words in case someone willing to listen arrives unexpectedly one day; you never know, you might be able to share your experiences with others, and you must always be prepared. As to the end of all this, here is what we know: some say that just before the moment of your death you will be able to see the labyrinth from high above. Yes, as if you were a bird soaring the skies, if you happen to have seen a bird before and know what it is. And from that height you will finally find out where the exit is. But then, of course, it will be a pointless revelation, since trying to escape from the labyrinth at that point in time will prove to be unlikely. It comes too late! Although nobody knows whether there are other labyrinths nearby, with other inhabitants and other paths to follow, you are allowed to shout in case someone might hear you. We have, nevertheless, a strong suspicion that you are very much on your own, so that shouting inside the labyrinth would be comparable to shouting in deep space where nothing can be heard, and no sound can be reproduced. And yet shouting in a void is so much more convincing than the void on its own: if the wake of your screams remains, then at least something lives on...."

"...*aun cuando se conozca el laberinto como la palma de la mano, es preferible esta opción a la huida, ignorándose como se ignora lo que nos espera al otro lado, pues nadie, que se sepa, ha logrado escapar hasta ahora. Mejor lo malo conocido, aunque la tentación de evadirse sea del todo irresistible. Sí, mejor claudicar y no arriesgarse a fracasar en el intento. Para qué huir, dicen algunos, si no hay más que lo que hay. Para qué imaginar lo que no existe o soñar con lo que no puede conseguirse. Para qué esforzarse cuando todo esfuerzo es inútil, toda visión falsa, toda explicación disparatada, toda resistencia inútil. Y por eso, he aquí una última advertencia: en el caso de que no hayamos encontrado la salida (que no la encontraremos, claro) y ya no nos alcance, digamos, la vida (que no nos alcanzará, según está previsto), se aconseja postrarse en un rincón y hacer un recuento de los senderos recorridos aun cuando no hayan conducido a nada. Para consolarse, uno podría inventarse relatos sobre situaciones parecidas de las que no haya escapatoria, y luego memorizar esos relatos por si un día, imprevisible pero también improbablemente, alguien llegara dispuesto a escucharnos. Hay quien asegura que en el instante mismo que precede a la muerte puede verse el laberinto con vista de pájaro y, por lo tanto, se descubre de manera concluyente dónde está la salida; se trata de una revelación improductiva para manifestar que la huida es a la vez posible e imposible. Aunque no se tengan noticias de que haya otros laberintos en las proximidades, con otros habitantes y otros trayectos, está permitido pedir socorro a voces por si alguien pudiera escucharnos. Pese a todo, se sospecha que uno existe en solitario, de manera que gritar en el laberinto se asemejaría a gritar en el vacío donde nada se escucha o reproduce. Y sin embargo, un grito en el vacío es tanto más deseable que el vacío por sí solo: si queda la estela del grito, entonces queda algo..."*

She insisted that I did not have enough milk to feed the baby. She said it in front of everyone. In a loud voice. With a frown. Without any kind of understanding.

If you do not know the meaning of the word 'serenity', I can teach you by sitting very still beside you.

After a superb meal at one of the best restaurants near Dieppe, which we could hardly afford, we were all horribly sick on the ferry crossing the English Channel. *"¡La langosta no, la langosta no!"* Father could be heard shouting along the passenger deck, until he too succumbed.

And all this too shall pass, like all other things shall pass.

There is nothing extraordinary about writing, you are plainly a recording machine with an editing device, adding or subtracting as the case may be. You plunder the world and then select the best, and sometimes the worst, for full effect. Not a single sentence belongs to you, you little thief. And the expurgation is not yours either, for you beautify a text to convince others that what you say is true and to charm them with your borrowed or even stolen words, if that.

To give birth was to condemn someone to death, I concluded. It was a statement that I firmly came up with in my teens, but later on renounced with tremendous conviction and I did otherwise by procreating. The urge to reproduce was so much more powerful than my beliefs: sheer biology is head and shoulders above philosophy of any kind; fundamentally, it runs the world.

Yes, like Father had once defended his hill, I defended mine singlehandedly. I led people to believe that I had the support of many, a whole battalion of fictional warriors; and just like Father, I was all on my own with make-believe weapons that made me look like an omnipotent woman who could deal with whatever was thrown my way. This illusion does not mean, though, that the battle is completely lost or that I am utterly defeated or that I am not spirited enough in my own way.

She never did look back after that, as if the country of her birth had become but a signposting on the road, a stamp on an envelope.

A mental health expert cannot help you if you do not want to harm yourself or others, they said. And I asked: So, you only help those with suicidal or murderous tendencies? We would not put it exactly like that, they replied.

I am delving deeper in the past, intergenerationally speaking, so I can tell stories from long ago. This is one way of entering into a dialogue with family members who lived before me, mainly the women who had no say and whose stories were considered of no relevance by mainstream History, so that I can categorically state that they did not live or die in vain.

I need to research Father's life so much more. This will be my next book.

In hindsight, I should have dedicated my life only to motherhood. Or perhaps only to work. Or perhaps only to contemplative practice. You cannot be and do everything; but if you concentrate on only one pursuit, you will be blamed for the demise of all the others.

JFK Airport, end of September 2001. My flight is one of the first ones after the tragedy. Even here the air reeks of burnt tyres, there is trepidation in the air, people look at me suspiciously. I totally love NY but not this way. Streets and cars and shop interiors are all covered with the same silvery dust. But it is not dust, no. Everywhere the DNA spilt from the Towers fill the streets; I am nothing but a mass grave. Should I shake away these sacred human remains from my arms and hair? Just like this human dust, the burden of the terrible crime cascades on every one of us.

My first ever insurance broker phoned me late one evening. I was very young, and he was very drunk. His wife had been taken to hospital, about to give birth, and he felt overwhelmed by it all. While we spoke, he was doing something with the hand that was not holding the handset. I did not hang up immediately and instead tried to talk some sense into him. I felt pity, I suppose; but eventually I put down the phone down, and the next day I stopped the insurance policy going through. In time, I learnt not to waste my pity, and especially my time, on the underserving, the abusive, the wild, the corrupt.

"Speak properly, Isabel!" I shouted several times when I was having a stroke, giving myself orders I could not obey, my voice sounding like uncontrollable thunder. After the event and back at home from hospital, I stumbled over my words, though people benignly said that my speech sounded just fine. My mental health was affected as well: low mood, brain fog, memory loss and forgetfulness, and at darker times anxiety, fretfulness and even suicidal thoughts. I am overcoming all this gradually, but there is something here to stay: I now think in an entirely different way, my reasoning patterns have changed, I feel angrier and wilder, I tend to say and do things that I would not say and do before, I interpret language with very different connotations. I assume that in the process of remodelling itself after the strokes, the brain is forced to create a new identity in order to survive as an organ and continue living. I am yet to be introduced to this new me. Will we be able to get on, is the question to ask.

I finally wrote a novel, and later on I wrote several more, longer or shorter. This first novel took over two decades to write, not that during that time I did nothing but write it, of course. It turned out to be a highly intricate process; technically indeed, but more so personally. I suffered, yes, in both mind and body because of the length of the project (mentally, with stress; physically, with all kinds of psychosomatic ills). But once it was over and done with, I concluded that writing a novel was definitely not out of my reach. It was fear mostly that had stopped me from embarking on such a journey which, catastrophising as usual, I had anticipated as a quest from which I might not come out alive. In the end, a novel is yet one more story to tell; albeit a long and arduous one. I suppose this is the main reason novels are not written: the necessary hours and dedication. You need a lot of precious time to erect that momentous edifice of a story, all of which forces you to put your many other projects on hold, both the personal and the otherwise literary. No, you do not come out of it unscathed, but severely tarnished by all those fictional characters and their fictitious actions, almost as much as by some of the real characters in your life and their rotten exploits.

Lamenting the past: that memory should wither is not about oblivion taking over a life, but more about things becoming irrelevant. I deny my bouts of absent-mindedness with outbursts of unfamiliar emotions, as if I had been falsely accused of a crime. Even love seems to be forsaken, for I can no longer locate within me all those intense and fervent longings that used to make me swoon when thinking about the one I loved. Thus, gone is the exhilaration that used to preside over our lives, gone are the bright days that gave us hope.

Ah, the war. It was a civil war, was it not? People used to ask about it incessantly. I never want to talk about the war, Father would always say, rubbing his back at the same time. The memory of the war made his back itch, especially just below his right shoulder blade. That whole area had been scooped out when a grenade was thrown at him by a soldier from the opposing army. Most definitely a soldier from the next village, or someone related to him, or someone who had no intention of ever injuring a fly. Well, you know what civil wars are like, some would say to him. But do I, Father used to reply, do I know what a civil war is like, having fought one myself?

When I produced a memorable radio programme on the UK elections for the evening transmission, he raised his head and looked at me with suspicious eyes, strongly rubbing his nose because his nervous tick was now totally out of control. "So, you are not just a pretty face," he said in English, and made me cry.

The only Shakespearean role I ever performed in English secondary school was that of Miranda. I would learn the role pacing up and down the corridor at home for weeks. On the day of the performance, remembering the lines was not the problem; the problem arose from having to recite such formidable words when I was so much in awe of them: "O, wonder! How many goodly creatures are there here! How beauteous mankind is! O brave new world, that has such people in't."

A mystique was born around her, for she was not always visible, attainable, available.

No, none of us could believe what happened. We were expecting Washington DC for sure. Yes, Father's next commission would have been the US capital, where he would commendably shine and Mother would get what she had always desired, an even more prominent life. As it was, instead of a career in Washington, Father was exiled to the coldest town in the nation. Instead of fame and glory to Father, metastasis to Mother. It must have been the shock, the shame, the unfairness of it all, the consequences of living under a most horrifying political regime that could so easily turn against its own. It was death to Mother, and the destruction of our family. Even at the end of his life, Father thought that his exile had been nothing but an administrative error, a case of mistaken identity, an entirely humourless joke.

Like Henry Miller, I am now ready to become an unacknowledged watercolourist.

There were two routes home from my secondary girls' school in Madrid, the longer one through the high street, and the shorter one through narrow and dark streets. If we were in a hurry, I would take the second route; but the boys from a local school knew this and would wait for us. You could run, but they would run faster. It was always the same routine: one of the members of the group of boys would be encouraged to run after you, with clapping, whistling and shouting from all the others. Once the boy reached you, he would put his hand up your skirt and into your pants and touch you all the way. However, on one occasion I laughed instead of screaming: it was when a boy performed the usual heinous act whilst I was on my period, and his hand come out dripping with blood, a look of total horror on his face.

What would become of her if it were the other way round: that she had so very few things to do and so very much time.

He cannot understand how I can have no roots, am tied by no customs, follow few traditions, show little interest in matters relating to king and country. I am a citizen of the world, I keep replying to him, though I admit this does sound rather contrived and grandiose. Perhaps I should say that I am just a citizen, of no particular abode, and certainly of no specific faith or lifestyle. Had I been asked to choose, I would have probably wanted to be like him: a nice upbringing in a family with roots going back a long time, with heirlooms dating to olden days, with a huge chorus of like-minded voices supporting and encouraging my every move and belief so that I would feel part of a closely-knit family, town, country. But then, you see, I had no choice whatsoever in the small, unimportant matter of my life.

Mother would repeat this regularly, and I suppose I needed constant repetition so that I would hold back my true desires: *"Sé discreta, que no sepan lo que estás pensando, que nadie te conozca."* I suppose that writing a memoir is ultimately an act of rebellion against Mother.

As heard at the London Book Fair: *"¿Sigues escribiendo?"* He asked that, but what I heard was: "Are you still breathing?" As I did not reply, the uninspired assistant to my old publisher repeated his question even louder.

It does happen sometimes that you get to meet your rapist once again, thirty years later. He contacted me through a common friend, who is understandably not my friend any longer. I was reluctant to meet him at first, mostly because I would be betraying my younger self. But I thought that I might just be able to make a formal complaint against him after all, historical as the crime was. An expert told me, however, that it would be difficult to prove a decades-old accusation, which in any case I did not denounce at the time for there was little evidence even then. And despite this piece of advice, I agreed to meet my rapist. I was curious as to how he had turned out, and perhaps I could include him *verbatim* as one of the despicable characters in the book I was writing –the attraction of acquiring a new angle on human nature is sometimes irresistible despite the risk and the abhorrence. Expressly, the idea was to use him as he had once used me. So, we met in a restaurant, surrounded by lots of people as witnesses of any potential and renewed attacks. Moments after sitting down at our table, he half-heartedly apologised for what had happened years earlier, not that I had forgotten or forgiven, and had no desire to do either; moreover, I firmly take an eye-for-an-eye stance, nothing less. By the end of the meal, over dessert, he confessed the real purpose of the meeting: not to ask for forgiveness but to enquire about my availability. What are you talking about, I asked in amazement. It turned out he was looking for a wife –yes, exactly that! His latest wife, like all his previous wives or partners, had left him and he wanted another one, all very simple really. I held back from striking out at him. And as I got up to leave, I roared that a crime cannot be erased with another crime. "What do you mean?" he whispered, as people sitting at other tables looked in our direction. And I replied in an even angrier tone of voice: You are entertaining the primeval idea that a rapist should marry the woman he raped, as if this were a noble act that would somehow placate her and erase the crime! And then I left the restaurant without looking back, for there was really nothing there to see, nothing at all, nothing whatsoever.

"Decíamos ayer" ("Dicebamus hesterna die"): its origin is not clear. Attributed to poet Fray Luis de León in 1577, who was prosecuted by the Inquisition because of his translation of the Song of Songs (*'Shir ha-Shirim'*) into vulgar language, he expressed the famous words when reinstated to the University of Salamanca. Philosopher Miguel de Unamuno also said those words when he was finally reinstated to his chair at the same university in 1930, after having been ousted during the dictatorship of Primo de

Rivera. Even I humbly used those words when returning to so-called 'normal life' after a lengthy period of recovery to reinstate both body and mind: *"Decíamos ayer."*

After the war, Mother wore the same dress for a long time. A single dress could cost several weeks' salary, so every month she would embellish it in a different way. This month a large bow and next month an embroidered flower. A red belt, a blue sash, a knitted bolero in pink. She would add frills to the skirt and make it a little longer or enhance it with a petticoat so it would be fully flared. Long or short sleeves, three-quarter sleeves, no sleeves. Her dress was unrecognizable from one month to the next, cleverly transmuting into a new outfit each time. From what I can see in the pictures I have of Mother, she always looked striking in that single dress, smiling and clearly joyful. And look at me today, with my many dresses and my despondency.

Do you really want to wake up in the middle of the night and switch on your mobile and arouse its disturbing blue light and write down –either by jotting your words under 'Notes' or by sending yourself an email– a sentence, a description or a scene that suddenly and fully invades your mind like a swarm of locusts would and will not leave you alone for a second, shouting their message at full force until you take notice of them and pay the attention such ideas think they deserve? I know that Lewis Carroll invented a device to write in the dark, and I must look further into this. A nyctograph is the name, with its very own alphabet, like a type of shorthand. The language of the night, we could sensibly call it.

A WOMAN ALONE

You are here solely to be loved by me, he said by way of a declaration.

Royal Warrant of Appointment: Great-grandfather was the official hatter of the then Spanish King, so that you know. When he died, so many of the inhabitants of Valladolid attended the wake in his home, as he was a much loved and respected figure in the city. Rumour has it that the King himself was also in attendance, though very much in disguise. The wake started with my great-grandmother and her four daughters (one of them my Grandmother) weeping in desperation. After large quantities of *jerez y bizcochos* had been served and consumed, the wake ended with all attendees telling some very offensive jokes in front of the open coffin and laughing animatedly, probably also in desperation.

Sex on the first date cuts short the courting and the flirting, and so they were never friends but became lovers without going through the comradeship stage. The connection between them was founded on little to go by, and the flirting game was up almost immediately, as it usually is. They were never able to discuss what afflicted them because they had not created a language for it and, even worse, feelings were never incorporated into the discussion but were instead considered foreign and unnecessary. It was a connection of sorts, with two highly critical individuals probing every word and move posed by the other, trying to defend their position and retain their territory. And despite all, it was what you could call a loving relationship.

At school, B had a kind of slave, a fag, doing things for him, giving B money or items of stationery he owned, picking up the pieces after fights, trying to replace any broken objects in school, collecting stuff like stamps or stickers for him. When B and I met, he tried the same approach with me. In my case, he called me not a slave but *"la mujer de su vida"* so that I would not object.

And when she finally comes to grips with everything that has happened, it is almost time to go.

Whilst at university and after having left Father's home, I decide to go and live with a boyfriend of sorts. Concealing my non-marital status, I inspect a few flats for rent. *"Calor y cariño"* someone says, showing me a dark and damp apartment without any source of natural light, a single bed professing to be double –for hot and suffocating nights. I see 10-12 properties perhaps and end up renting the smallest one on the fifth floor of an 18th century building, no lift. It requires so much more than just a lick of paint. A small door in the kitchen leads to an irrelevant toilet. There is no hot water in the apartment, just a single cold-water tap above the kitchen sink. Instead of despairing, I seek a solution: I will heat water in a small stove that feeds on a gas cylinder, and I will wash my body in a large tub. After much discussion with my boyfriend, we agree to rent the flat and begin to live together. The worst thing is that we have to get used to each other, which demands far too many concessions and proves to be intolerably hard. Love is only perfect when untouched and unlived, and I will have to learn about this the hard way. But for now, my main concern is that we need to replace the gas cylinder every week. At least we have electricity in the property, but it blacks out every now and then, so we must not overload the circuits. We must live frugally, carefully. We are used to being frugal and careful, this is a dictatorship after all. Or to put it in simpler terms, this is a political aberration where they know everything about you: your name, your address, your affiliation, probably whether you are living in sin, if you have no central gas supply where you live, if you have to wash in a tub. Luckily this fifth-floor apartment is bright and airy to a fault. All windows are facing a tiny inner yard onto which the sun shines for several hours a day, even in winter, and where you can hear the neighbours make mischief. At night, the neighbour from the second floor beats up his wife and child. The woman on the third-floor sings *zarzuela* at dawn to no one in particular. Medical students share an apartment on the ground floor and ask each other questions about bronchitis, conjunctivitis, peritonitis, all of them rising to our fifth floor. To some of those clinical questions I know the answers from my own experience. The very old lady who lives in the apartment next to us spends her day cleaning it. I have never seen her without an apron, in her hand a duster at all times; her pitiable abode shines as if made of gold. There is a retired actor on our floor. On his death, we have to attend the wake in his apartment. His open coffin is dramatically placed at a 45-degree angle for effect. As theatrical performances go, it is a great one. Throughout each episode I pretend I am married; my boyfriend pretends he is married. Everyone in the building thinks we are married, but they might be pretending as well. They would be upset if they knew that my boyfriend and I were in an extramarital relationship; in fact, we would not have been allowed to rent the apartment, customs here are still a century behind most European countries. Friends come and see us occasionally, but they think hard about climbing five floors to get to where we live. I had nothing better to do today, my best friend says on arrival. I suppose friendship must be based on sincerity. In the summer, my boyfriend and I are away from each other for almost a month. When he returns, I get something I do not want. Instead of blaming him, I blame myself. I say sorry, I must have caught this STD from somewhere: from the air itself, from sitting in public lavatories, on the bus, the tube, someone's car. He says nothing to my comments; my feelings towards him begin to wane. What else is there for me to do: I fall in love with a classmate from my Politics class. He is kind and fine-looking and has the bluest eyes. I wonder if the infatuation is due to the powerful medication I am taking. Love can happen regardless of circumstances, in the strangest of places, at the most inconvenient times. I tell all to my boyfriend, even though the blue-eyed boy does not seem to love me in return. My boyfriend's idea that he would be the only man for me throughout my life is now in tatters. We say goodbye, and that is the end of that, sadly or happily who can say. I leave the house, but I have nowhere to go. On the main road I stick my thumb out and a Citroën with three young men stops. I am trying to put it all behind me, but I should know better; I have been through this on untold occasions, getting into a stranger's car. This time I might come out of it unharmed; in fact, I am intent on it. It is a given right to confront and demand; yet for any new strategy women wish to deploy, we need numbers; and we do not have them just yet, though very soon we will.

Should you avoid showing an inch of vulnerability and put on instead your resting-bitch face so that no one can hurt you?

It was not to last. After further radiotherapy, there was a little lump behind the ear. Again, Mother pointed it out to me, and I felt it with my index finger: hard, round, perfect, like a tiny plum waiting to ripen. The lump was removed in due course, but those were the days when not much was done about the aesthetics of it all, mostly because cosmetic surgery was in its infancy. Mother's face dropped to one side by what felt like half a mile. One flank was her usual patrician self; the other showed a crestfallen woman, unable to smile, let alone laugh. She was half a person already by then.

And on that very cold and snowy day they went for a stroll along Chiswick Bridge, and from the railings she removed her wedding ring and tossed it all the way into the icy waters of the river. Am I free from him now? she said, shivering and wet. They got back into the car, and she cried in silence, wondering whether she had ended one difficult relationship only to get herself into a much shoddier one.

I walked for miles without stopping once. I should have timed myself and measured the distance, you never know when you can break a record. I even forgot to eat. I only had a cup of tea first thing in the morning, and another cup when I got home around midnight. It is not something I did on purpose, I assure you. Only when I got home did I realise what had happened. I sat down and struggled to remember, step by step. At first, I vaguely recalled the original cup of tea. Then it all came back to me: opening the door; following the alleyway leading to the park; walking all the way there and all the way back; eventually getting home so very late. But as hard as I tried, I could not remember in minute detail what had taken place between leaving home and returning, though I must have gone through quite a lot for me to look so old.

"¡Podría haber sido peor!": it was her mantra and, most of the time, mine.

In the second week of December, Mother was allowed to come home from hospital. It would be her last Christmas. I went out shopping with her along the high street to buy presents for my younger siblings. The Christmas spirit did nothing to cheer me up, but she was herself excited to be going back to normal life, albeit so very briefly. With a bright and colourful silk scarf she covered one side of her face, the one damaged beyond repair after the operation to remove the cyst behind her ear. But the scarf kept slipping, and after a while she gave up and showed everyone what she looked like. The destruction was visible on the good side as well; it was probably the snowballing soreness she undoubtedly felt all over her body. Those who knew the family would stop and stare in the street, and some dared to ask Mother, looking at the scar on her face and the facial muscles that had been displaced sideways, whether she was home to stay. She replied, trying to exude enthusiasm; no, she would never admit defeat, ever, and said that she was very happy to be home and that it was so lovely to get back to normal life. *"Tan contenta!"* Counselling was unheard of at the time, and patients were not told what they were suffering from, perhaps to make doctors' jobs less trying. After Christmas she was asked to go back to hospital. Those very civil doctors said euphemistically to Mother that she had a case of pleurisy and that she needed to recover. They explained that she had caught cold when leaving the operating theatre, blatantly lying. And after New Year she was back in her hospital room, and from there to the right hospital department to deal with the supposed pleurisy, that pretend ailment. They stuck a needle into her lungs and out came a thick yellow liquid into a large glass container on the floor. I was with her and saw the procedure, which I later learnt had been pointless but was meant to stop her from knowing the truth. What was, I wonder, that viscous and puzzling liquid. Nothing to do with pleurisy and probably everything to do with the big C. The habitat of a monster. The lagoon where a dark creature lived. The damage done to healthy lungs by some horrific beast. By then, all hell was breaking lose. Metastasis, as the concluding invasion of a body, was affirming itself. The very final conflict. The end of the end. The last lap of all. Yes, as I said earlier it was Mother's last Christmas. And in a way, it was my last Christmas as well, because after that I did not wish to celebrate the occasion ever again. And if I did kind of celebrate Christmas in due course, it was for the sake of others who enjoyed those festivities so much more than I ever could. I detest any such celebrations –to celebrate exactly what?

What is there not to love about a man who grows pink roses just for you?

We are in Bregenz and have just seen the remarkable Weinstein opera set in Auschwitz. After the performance we walk along the bowels of the theatre to exit the opera house and return to the hotel, still shaken by the haunting drama. A member of the chorus has left the stage and walks hurriedly in our direction, probably going to the dressing room to change into his real clothes and leave behind his terrifying role for a few hours before the next performance. He is clothed as a Nazi officer, marching at speed, still in character. When I see him approaching us, I scream like no one had screamed on stage. It was like perfectly remembering something that had not exactly happened to me but so easily could have.

Just an idea: staying away from everyone and everything has all the advantages of death and none of its disadvantages.

And Dr W was my first contact with the world of the sensual. Me, a pre-adolescent, sitting on a dentist's chair and enveloped by this very huge man who smelt of ether and who wanted to find out what my toothache was all about.

H is one of my oldest friends and she calls me to say that my ex-boyfriend wants to kill himself because I threw him out of my life. She says that he phoned her and wept desperately, persuading her that he was the victim, not me. I remember that my ex-boyfriend could cry at the drop of a hat, on command, with large and perfectly synchronised tears, while making strange bawling sounds and uttering cheaply poetic words. I fell for his ways for a while; and after we parted, he used the same method with my friends. When H phones me to intercede on his behalf, I tell her to piss off and mind her own business. And that really makes her cry in the very real sense of the word.

Ciudadano Dossier was a monthly feminist magazine in Francoist Spain, possibly the very first one. But at the time the term *feminist* was anathema, and so the subtitle of the magazine was *Hacia la igualdad de la mujer*, which was close enough. Although I worked there as a freelance because I was still a student at university, at one point I was appointed as a replacement sub-editor when one of the staff members went on maternity leave. For my job, I would interview feminist lawyers, talk openly about female and feminist issues, check out how things were progressing for women in that callous regime. And there is a picture of me at the printers of the magazine, sitting at a large table, tearing out a page; you can see how all the editorial team met up that night, all night, ripping a page from the current issue. This is what happened: the cartoon on the last page was that of a judge who had made suggestive remarks to a woman, based on a story which had actually taken place in a court of law. The orders came to our editor from above: either we pulped the whole issue, or we had to get rid of the cartoon by tearing out the relevant page before the magazine was sold in newsagents or sent out to subscribers. Thus, thousands of magazines were pruned and sanitised for our oppressed readers. Freedom of expression existed only in our wildest dreams.

And that year we went on holiday to the beach and Mother would insist on wearing a bikini. One cup filled with flesh, the other heaving with some kind of home-made stuffing that would show when she leaned forward to pick up her towel. What was displayed was a flat, darkened patch of skin, treated by radiotherapy and thoroughly burnt out, alongside the fleshful bounty of a perfectly formed breast.

According to epigenetics, I was produced not by my mother but by the mother of my mother. Yes, my mother's eggs were created by Grandmother, a woman who lived a life of privilege until it was all taken away: with a husband who lost his business; with the sole desire to be an artist but having to stick to colouring black and white postcards with aniline dyes; dedicated to the rearing of children with such very few means; living through a horrifying war and trying frantically to make ends meet. And then my mother produced me after having lived through the war, still struggling and hungry, in a devastated country with an even more devastating political system lasting decades. I was the result of her own life experience, me and my eggs. And my children were thus tainted, the fruit of my tortured mother. Is destiny purely biological, and can you do nothing to change your luck? Can you? Must you?

Therefore, how much of her life has she not lived because, to put it very simply, she was not mindfully there?

Aged six, watching Disney's 'Sleeping Beauty' at a Madrid cinema: it was my first and most precious contact with Tchaikovsky. Yet for a film meant for children, they advertised 'The Mummy' during the break. In those days there used to be breaks in the middle of films, with trailers announcing what would soon be shown in that cinema. I was thus presented with a choice: close my eyes or watch that chilling trailer. As I could still hear the sound from the trailer, I decided to open my eyes and watch everything thrown my way: both the sweetness of 'Sleeping Beauty' alongside the terror of 'The Mummy'. Would everything be both beautiful and deadly from now on, I asked myself then.

It was one way of saying that her marriage to Father was an unhappy one, but I did not understand the word *pedrea* until much later, when I learnt that it referred to a small prize in a lottery. *"El matrimonio es una lotería y a mí me ha tocado la pedrea,"* Mother used to say when Father was not around.

You cannot hide melancholy. A friend I had been in touch with on the phone but whom I had never met, said immediately upon seeing me in the flesh: *"Eres muy guapa, pero tienes los ojos tristes."*

A very public notice: Absolutely no bullying will be tolerated –at any time and under any circumstance and with any excuse– from bosses, colleagues, associates, allies, friends, acquaintances, partners, family members, and even from her own children.

On my daily walk along the park, I suddenly see it. From afar, it looks like a pile of something square, solid, colourful. And as I approach the object, I realise it is a collection of three boxed sets of vinyl LPs. Nobody uses those anymore, even I disposed of my old record-player a long time ago. What is worse is that they are basically easy listening LPs from some years back and not my style at all: 'Quiet Music for Quiet Listening', 'Country Magic' and 'Orchestral Magic'. The three sets have been left to their own fate, and I feel sorry for any discarded object that could still be put to good use, even if it is not-so-great music and the vinyl must probably be scratched, and I no longer have a record-player. When I pick up the three sets, I realise they smell of damp and age, and must have been in someone's basement for a long time. My, they are heavy, each box containing several records, I am sure they weigh over five kilogrammes, probably much more. I now remember that I am deep in the park, probably around two and a half miles from home. All these calculations of weight and distance disrupt my mind and stress me. I must plan a strategy, not only about the distance to get home but also about how to carry the weight. I am not that strong anymore, not that resilient or steady. Despite all, I pick up the three sets and off I go. And as I begin to walk with my prize (it is a prize or just a burden, I begin to wonder) I look around and into the distance, because those LPs must belong to someone. Perhaps the owner left them there to take a rest and would return for them later. Or perhaps that person did not want them anymore and instead of placing them in the recycling bin decided nonsensically to leave them in the park. Or were those LPs a secret sign, as in a spy yarn. Or where they a loving gift for someone, as in a romantic tale. Or were they left specifically there to signpost a location, like clues left all over the park as in a game of hide and seek. Or is it a prank, and someone is filming me from far away, a woman in black carrying those heavy items with enormous difficulty all along the park. No, definitely no one goes for a walk in the park and comes back carrying a collection of old easy-listening LPs. Except me, of course. Only I would be capable of such folly, I conclude.

And as it was, this colleague of mine displayed his loathing by openly calling me *Doña Perfecta*.

"Oh, I did not realise you had published this book called *'Dolorem Ipsum'*," he says. "Yes, it is my most recent book and I published it during the pandemic," she replies, "and the image on the cover is from Strasbourg Cathedral, a picture I took when visiting the city some years ago; let me show you all the other images and some of the poems." And before she even gets to open the book, he leaves the room.

"Si no lo veo, no lo creo." Father, a profoundly pious man, would regularly make such rational statements, thus contradicting everything he stood for.

That day in hospital she asked me to wash and comb her hair. I was dismayed, more against myself than her. It was with so much trepidation that I touched her locks, washed them, dried them, put them in curlers. On her part, she was clearly uncomfortable as I was doing all that for her. She had always shown a strange kind of antagonism towards me, and I never managed to find out why. Perhaps she still held against me the uttermost pain I had caused her when she gave birth to me, that premature and breech baby.

And echoing Bartleby, I replied: "I would prefer not to."

Some women might never be able to pee properly and, we could say, flowingly. In public lavatories there is no denying anything: you can clearly distinguish between the sounds produced by those who spontaneously tore their perineum during childbirth, and those who had an episiotomy done by a professional with a shiny scalpel to enlarge the baby's exit route. I have experienced both, a ripped flesh wound and a clean surgical cut, and I do not recommend either.

For any sort of profession, but particularly for this one, you have to fulfil certain requirements: you must be on a permanent state of alert; you need heightened powers of observation to pick up signals in others, anything subliminal must not escape you, like a single flick of the eye or any squirming of the mouth; you must pretend that you are not studying anyone's facial expressions carefully so as not to offend or disturb; you must be both detached yet at the same time heavily involved in every event without anyone noticing; you must prove to be exceptionally sentient even though others will claim that you live in the clouds; you must never confess that you are in fact scrutinising someone's mind when having long and banal conversations with them; ultimately, you should never let them know what you are really up to .

Grandfather and books: *"No hay ningún libro que sea malo, porque de todos los libros se puede aprender."*

The thieving nanny, in all her guilt, came back into my life. The look of absolute fear concealed by an awkward smile gave her away when I met her momentarily at a shopping centre. Then I did not see her again for several decades. And suddenly one day, by chance, I learnt about her. A friend of mine mentioned her, and I said that she had been our nanny but revealed nothing about the theft. I was now aware of where she lived and what had become of her, married as she with a child as she was now. I did not know how to proceed and which course of action to embark on: accuse her publicly, call the police, take her to court. There is no proof, there are no witnesses. Just like in a case of rape, my intimate possessions had been violated, and there was nothing I could do to restore justice. And all these years later, I just want her to reply to a few questions: Did she feel guilt or shame when stealing my family jewels? Did she sell those precious items at a handsome price? What did she spend the money on? Drugs, drink, sex? Should she rot, should she suffer? And the most important question, should she be forgiven after all this time?

We could well talk about a mussitation of novelists, a susurration of poets, an aspiration of playwrights, a reminiscence of memoirists.

If there is a school of thought that we were educated in as children, it was the so-called *sentimiento trágico de la vida*, not so much based on the renowned essay by Unamuno (stating that life is tragic because of our urge to be immortal and our struggle to evade death), but on a pious standpoint. Thus, these famous words were borrowed from the eximious writer and used extensively to prop up distorted views, with most people not realising the connection to his work; to talk about a 'tragic sense of life' certainly imbues any obtuse ideas with qualities that they might not otherwise have. In its conventional usage, and not in the sense given to such words by the renowned author, this 'tragic sense of life' refers to the darkness of certain religious beliefs and rituals, all based on the misery, torture and death of their highest leader. It views events as disasters, existence as unapologetically dark, and suffering as the proper and rightful way of life. Thus, we were taught that living is nothing but a tragedy, and to think otherwise a sin; this is to say, to be joyful does not make for a serious and virtuous existence. My apologies for the digression, but I wanted to explain that I have included the closing words of this admirable work by Unamuno at the very end of the memoir, for there are no greater words with which to close a book, and I could not come up with anything equally appropriate.

On certain days there is no other option but to proceed with a manic sense of urgency, without giving it another thought, caution left behind, with no consideration for prudence or reflection. Blink, hesitate momentarily, take a short breath and you will miss it all. It is either now or never. And the time is, and always will be, precisely now.

"¡Nunca serás feliz!" said Mother. *"¿Por qué?"* I asked aged ten. And she said that it was because I was always complaining: *"Siempre estás quejándote."* Does this mean that the secret to happiness is to avoid grumbling about everything and to stop the complaints and the objections and the negativity? Not for a moment, that would be far too easy an explanation about unhappiness. But I have always wondered whether what Mother said was more a curse than a piece of advice: *"¡Nunca serás feliz!"*

After she died, the first thing I did was to go to the chemist and buy medication for my agonising periods. The product had the eeriest name, Saldeva (or *'Sal de Eva'*). It contained probably nothing more than aspirin, but it was obvious from its name that it was a remedy for women's issues. Oh, my menses were as painful as childbirth, as I would find out when giving birth years later. For a few days a month I was totally out of action, as if taking a break from normal life; sometimes I was even sent home from school. I have already mentioned that Mother never allowed me to take anything for my painful menstruation. But now that she was no longer alive, I could finally do whatever I wanted to stop this horrid, beastly pain. I went to the local pharmacy to ask for medication to help me in my plight. And there I was in front of the assistant pharmacist, who opened her mouth when she saw me but did not say anything for a few seconds as if trying to pinpoint who I was. She was a young woman, a girl not much older than me, and she finally realised who I was and said that she not seen my mother for a long time: *"¿Cómo está tu madre?"* And I replied: *"Está muerta."* I said it coldly, in a matter-of-fact way. How else could I say it; what else was there to say; what emotions should I display for someone else's sake? Should one produce a special tone of voice, a dark gaze, a fleeting tear? I remained motionless and showed not an ounce of feeling. I simply wanted to make the announcement of a fact and get it quickly out of the way. Why make a big thing? It annoyed me so much to be asked. Death was a simple enough event, it happened to everyone, there was nothing exceptional about it. In any case, I was in the pharmacy to buy medication, not to talk about the dead and the particular circumstances of their passing. But the assistant pharmacist, perhaps the type of woman I would possibly aspire to be within a few years (why ever could I not become a pharmacist's assistant?), began to weep loudly and uncontrollably; luckily there was no one else in the pharmacy at the time. A stream of tears flowed from her eyes like a spring, and she blushed intensely. She went on sobbing and saying nothing, but from her flickering gaze it was obvious that she was seeing moving images of every occasion when Mother had been in that pharmacy and of all the products she had ever bought there. Of course, not all the medication in the world could have served Mother one bit to fight the fiend that had taken over her body and finally destroyed her. And for quite a long while the woman did nothing but cry, as if I was not there; perhaps she was crying for all the things that she had not ever cried for before. I thought her crying would never end, but I said not a single thing to comfort her. When I walked towards the door to the street, she was still whimpering. I was surprised by my own detached reaction, not wanting to interact, feeling unsympathetic about the whole thing, thinking things like: "Hold on, this is my mother's death we are talking about, what right do you have to cry so desperately about it. I am the protagonist in this story, and you are a mere spectator. It is my show, my tragedy. Be quiet, woman, it is not a death that you will have to deal with, but I will." As I left the pharmacy, I looked back briefly, in my hand a small paper bag with the medication I so desperately needed to alleviate my period pain. Between all the crying and lamenting, I had managed to squeeze in my request and had finally bought my longed-for medication.

Cicero said something similar: with a library and a garden, you cannot go wrong.

Recapping: she told her story as she recalled it, so the narration was very much her version of events. There might have been empty expanses, moments of silence, incomplete renderings and, of course, other sides to the story itself. But about such things, there was nothing she could do.

La danse and *La musique* were stolen from our local silversmith. Mother had sent the two little antique sculptures there for silverplating. With their name etched on the base, they were originally in my room (I was both a dancer and a musician at that young age, and the sculptures had been a present from Mother). I never saw Mother sadder than when she learnt about the theft. Apparently, the value of all the stolen items in the shop, many others as well as ours, ran into the thousands, which in those days amounted to quite a fortune. There was the customary police investigation, and the employees at the silversmiths were all interviewed. Neither the investigation nor the interviews got anywhere. Stolen goods exchange hands far too quickly, we were officially told, and nothing could be done to recover them. Someone stole them, someone sold them, someone bought them, and someone sold them once more. Probably several times over. And that was the end of that. We never heard about our little sculptures ever again. Except that right now, they are on someone's mantlepiece, I am quite certain of that. Just in case, please check. They are two female figures representing the two highest arts, Music and Dance. If so, please return them at your earliest convenience. You have had them long enough by now, and I have sadly lived without them for most of my life. When I remember this episode, I want to cry but never do; I think it is because the theft of the sculptures may account for the fact that I became neither a dancer nor a musician despite my childhood dreams to be both. I could well say that I now dance to the music of words, but it is best to keep this sort of comment to myself.

"What is the worst side effect of the medication I have to take every day?" I asked. And without looking up, they replied: "Death!"

Did I achieve what I wanted to achieve? Well, for one thing the end is mercifully not yet here, so there is time for what I still need to do, and hopefully plenty of time. Yes, the outcome of all this may not be what I anticipated, nor have I become the person I set out to be. But I did manage a few encouraging results, undeniably so; I am not sure whether it was because I was running out of steam and had to inevitably settle for what I already had, or whether it was because I rightly managed to fight it out. In the process, I must admit that a few exciting territories have been discovered, some interesting questions posed, a number of useless cups broken.

A poem that I wrote in my early twenties could have easily been the very last one: *"esta cordura... / entre luces y sombras he crecido / escribiendo mensajes en el agua, / sin elegir me quedo, / observo que la vida es / un ave velocísima, / la lucidez del último momento"*

As Welles so luminously asserted: if you want a happy ending, that very much depends on where you would like to stop the story.

And this is my shot at *sangfroid*: I do not know what I could have done differently.

Miguel de Unamuno: *"Espero, lector, que mientras dure nuestra tragedia, en algún entreacto, volvamos a encontrarnos. Y nos reconoceremos. Y perdona si te he molestado más de lo debido e inevitable, más de lo que, al tomar la pluma para distraerte un poco de tus distracciones, me propuse."*

For what it is worth, I have spoken.

THE END

A WOMAN ALONE

© isabeldelrio 2021

Friends of Alice Publishing

ISBN - 978-1-9160306-8-8

Printed in Great Britain
by Amazon